Zone Policeman 88

Harry A. Franck

Table of Contents

Zone Policeman 88

Harry A. Franck

Kessinger Publishing reprints thousands of hard–to–find books!

Visit us at http://www.kessinger.net

ZONE POLICEMAN 88
A CLOSE RANGE STUDY OF THE PANAMA CANAL AND ITS WORKERS

TO A HOST OF GOOD FELLOWS THE ZONE POLICE

Quito, December 31, 1912

CHAPTER I

Strip by strip there opened out before me, as I climbed the "Thousand Stairs" to the red–roofed Administration Building, the broad panorama of Panama and her bay; below, the city of closely packed roofs and three–topped plazas compressed in a scallop of the sun–gleaming Pacific, with its peaked and wooded islands to far Taboga tilting motionless away to the curve of the earth; behind, the low, irregular jungled hills stretching hazily off into South America. On the third–story landing I paused to wipe the light sweat from forehead and hatband, then pushed open the screen door of the passageway that leads to police headquarters.

"Emm—What military service have you had?" asked "the Captain," looking up from the letter I had presented and swinging half round in his swivel–chair to fix his clear eyes upon me.

"None."

"No?" he said slowly, in a wondering voice; and so long grew the silence, and so plainly did there spread across "the Captain's" face the unspoken question, "Well, then what the devil are you applying here for?" that I felt all at once the stern necessity of putting in a word for myself or lose the day entirely.

"But I speak Spanish and—"

"Ah!" cried "the Captain," with the rising inflection of awakened interest, "That puts another face on the matter."

Slowly his eyes wandered, with the far–away look of inner reflection, to the vacant chair of "the Chief" on the opposite side of the broad flat desk, then out the wide–open window and across the shimmering roofs of Ancon to the far green ridges of the youthful Republic, ablaze with the unbroken tropical sunshine. The whirr of a telephone bell broke in upon his meditation. In sharp, clear–cut phrases he answered the questions that came to him over the wire, hung up the receiver, and pushed the apparatus away from him with a forceful gesture.

"Inspector:" he called suddenly; but a moment having passed without response, he went on in his sharp–cut tones, "How do you think you would like police work?"

"I believe I should."

2

"The Captain" shuffled for a moment one of several stacks of unfolded letters on his desk.

"Well, it's the most thankless damned job in Creation," he went on, almost dreamily, "but it certainly gives a man much touch with human nature from all angles, and—well, I suppose we do some good. Somebody's got to do it, anyway."

"Of course I suppose it would depend on what class of police work I got," I put in, recalling the warning of the writer of my letter of introduction that, "You may get assigned to some dinky little station and never see anything of the Zone,"—"I'm better at moving around than sitting still. I notice you have policemen on your trains, or perhaps in special duty languages would be—"

"Yes, I was thinking along that line, too," said "the Captain."

He rose suddenly from his chair and led the way into an adjoining room, busy with several young Americans over desks and typewriters.

"Inspector," he said, as a tall and slender yet muscular man of Indian erectness and noticeably careful grooming rose to his feet, "Here's one of those rare people, an American who speaks some foreign languages. Have a talk with him. Perhaps we can arrange to fix him up both for his good and our own."

"Ever done police duty?" began the Inspector, when "the Captain" had returned to the corner office.

"No."

"Military ser—"

"Nor that either."

"Well, we usually require it," mused the Inspector slowly, flashing his diamond ring, "but with your special qualifications perhaps—

"You'd probably be of most use to us in plain clothes," he continued, after a dozen questions as to my former activities; "We could put you in uniform for the first month or six weeks until you know the Isthmus, and then—

"Our greatest trouble is burglary," he broke off abruptly, rising to reach a copy of the "Canal Zone Laws"; "If you have nothing else on hand you might run these over; and the 'Police Rules and Regulations,'" he added, handing me a small, flat volume bound in light brown imitation leather.

I sat down in an arm–chair against the wall and fell to reading, amid the clickity–click of typewriters, telephone calls even from far–off Colon on the Atlantic, and the constant going and coming of a negro orderly in shiningly ironed khaki uniform. By and by the Inspector drifted into the main office, where his voice blended for some time with that of "the Captain," At length he came back bearing a copy of the day's Star and Herald, turned back to the "Estrella de Panama" pages so rarely opened in the Zone.

"Just run us off a translation of that, if you don't mind," he said, pointing to a short paragraph in Spanish.

Some two minutes later I handed him the English version of the account of a near–duel between two Panamanians, and took once more to reading. It was more than an hour later that I was again interrupted.

"You'll want to catch the 5:25 back to Corozal?" inquired the Inspector;" Mr.—–, give him transportation to Culebra and back, and an order for physical examination.

"You might fill out this application blank," he added, handing me a long legal sheet, "then in case you are appointed that much will be done."

The document began with the usual, "Name——, Birthplace——, and so on." There followed the information that the appointee "must be at least five feet eight; weigh one hundred and forty, chest at least thirty–four inches—" Then suddenly near the bottom of the back of the sheet my eyes caught the startling words;—"Unless you are sure you are a man of physical appearance far above the average do not fill out this application."

4

I was suddenly aware of a sinking feeling in the pit of my stomach; the blank all but slipped from my nerveless fingers. Then all at once there came back to me the words of some chance acquaintance of some far−off time and place, words which were the only memory that remained to me of the speaker, except that he had lived long and gathered much experience, "Bluff, my boy, is what carries a man through the world. Act as if you're sure you are and can and you'll generally make the other fellow think so." I sat down at a desk and filled out the application in my most self− confident flourish.

"Go to Culebra to−morrow," said the Inspector, as I bade the room good−day and stepped forth with my most military stride and bearing, "and report back here Friday morning."

I descended to the world below, not by the long perspective of stairs that leads down and across the gully to the heart of Ancon, but by a short−cut that took me quickly into a foreign land. The graveled highway at the foot of the hill I might not have guessed was an international boundary had I not chanced to notice the instant change from the trim, screened Zone buildings, each in its green lawn, to the featureless architecture of a city where grass is all but unknown; for the formalities of crossing this frontier are the same as those of crossing any village street. It was my first entrance into the land of the panamenos, technically known on the Zone as "Spigoties," and familiarly, with a tinge of despite, as "Spigs"; because the first Americans to arrive in the land found a few natives and cabmen who claimed to "Speaga dee Eng−leesh."

To Americans direct from the States Panama city ranks still as rather a miserable dawdling village. But that is due chiefly to lack of perspective. Against the background of Central America it seemed almost a great, certainly a flourishing, city. Even to−day there are many who complain of its unpleasant odors; to those who have lived in other tropical cities its scent is like the perfumes of Araby; and none but those can in any degree realize what "Tio Sam" has done for the place.

Toward sunset I passed through a gateway with scores of fellow− countrymen, all as composedly at home as in the heart of their native land. Across the platform stood a train distinctively American in every feature, a bilious−yellow train divided by the baggage car into two sections, of which the five second−class coaches behind the engine, with their wooden benches, were densely packed in every available space with workmen and laborer's wives, from Spaniards to ebony negroes, with the average color decidedly dark. In the first−class cars at the Panama end were Americans, all but exclusively white

5

Americans, with only here and there a "Spigoty" with his long greased hair, his finger rings, and his effeminate gestures, and even a negro or two. For though Uncle Sam may permit individual states to do so, he may not himself openly abjure before the world his assertion as to the equality of all men by enacting "Jim Crow" laws.

We were soon off. Settled back in the ample seat of the first real train I had boarded in months, with the roar of its length over the smooth and solid road–bed, the deep–voiced, masculine whistle instead of the painful, puerile screech that had recently assailed my ear, I all but forgot I was in a foreign land. The fact was recalled by the passing of the train–guard,—an erect and self– possessed young American in "Texas" hat, khaki uniform, and leather leggings, striding along the aisle with a jerking, half– arrogant swing of the shoulders. So, perhaps, might I too soon be parading across the Isthmus! It was not, to be sure, exactly the role I had planned to play on the Zone. I had come rather with the hope of shouldering a shovel and descending into the canal with other workmen, that I might some day solemnly raise my right hand and boast, "I helped dig IT." But that was in the callow days before I had arrived and learned the awful gulf that separates the sacred white American from the rest of the Canal Zone world. Besides, had I not always wanted to be a policeman and twirl a club and stalk with heavy, law–compelling tread ever since I had first stared speechless upon one of those noble beings on my first trip out into the world twenty–one years before?

It was not without effort that I rose in time next morning to continue on the 6:37 from Corozal across another bit of the Zone. Exactly thus should one first see the Great Work, piece–meal, slowly; unless he will go home with it all in an undigested lump. The train rolled across a stretch of almost uninhabited country, with a vast plain of broken rock on the right, plunged unexpectedly through a short tunnel, and stopped at a station perched on the edge of a ridge above a small Zone town backed by some vast structure, above which here and there a huge crane loomed against the sky of dawn. Another mile and the collectors were announcing as brazenly as if they challenged the few "Spigs" on board to correct them, "Peter M'Gill! Peter M'Gill!" We were already moving on again before I had guessed that by this noise they designated none other than the famous Pedro Miguel. The sun rose suddenly as we swung sharply to the left and rumbled across a girderless bridge. Barely had I time to discover that we were crossing the great canal itself and to catch a brief glimpse of the jagged gulf in either direction, before the train had left it behind, as if the sight of the world–famous channel were not worth a pause, and was roaring on through a hilly country of perpetual summer. A peculiarly shaped reservoir sped past on the left, twice or thrice more the green horizon rose and fell, and at 7:30 we drew up at the base of Culebra, the Zone capital.

On the screened veranda of a somewhat sooty and dismal building high up near the summit of the town, another and I were pacing anxiously back and forth when, well on in the morning, an abrupt and rather gloomy–faced American dashed into the building and one of the rooms thereof, snapping over his shoulder as he disappeared, "One of you!" The other had precedence. Then soon from behind the wooden shutters came a growl of "Next!" and two moments later I was standing in the reputed costume of Adam on the scales within. At about ten–second intervals a monosyllable fell from the lips of the morose American as he delved into my personal make–up from crown to toe with all the instrumental circumspection known to his secret–discovering profession. Then with a gruff "Dress!" he sat down at a table to scratch a few fantastic marks on the blank I had brought, and hand it to me as I caught up my last garment and turned to the door. But, alas—tight sealed! and all the day, though carrying the information in my pocket, I must live in complete ignorance of whether I had been found lacking an eye or a lung. For sooner would one have asked his future of the scowling Parques than venture to invoke a hint thereof from that furrow–browed being from the Land of Bruskness.

Meanwhile, as if it had been thus planned to give me such opportunity, I stood at the very vortex of canal interest and fame, with nearly an entire day before the evening train should carry me back to Corozal. I descended to the "observation platform." Here at last at my very feet was the famous "cut" known to the world by the name of Culebra; a mighty channel a furlong wide plunging sheer through "Snake Mountain," that rocky range of scrub–wooded hills; severing the continental divide. At first view the scene was bewildering. Only gradually did the eye gather details out of the mass. Before and beyond were pounding rock drills, belching locomotives, there arose the rattle and bump of long trains of flat–cars on many tracks, the crash of falling boulders, the snort of the straining steam–shovels heaping the cars high with earth and rock, everywhere were groups of little men, some working leisurely, some scrambling down into the rocky bed of the canal or dodging the clanging trains, all far below and stretching endless in either direction, while over all the scene hovered a veritable Pittsburg of smoke.

All long–heralded sights—such is the nature of the world and man —are at first glimpse disappointing. To this rule the great Culebra "cut" was no exception. After all this was merely a hill, a moderate ridge, this backbone of the Isthmus the sundering of which had sent its echoes to all corners of the earth. The long– fed imagination had led one to picture a towering mountain, a very Andes.

But as I looked longer, noting how little by comparison were the trains I knew to be of regulation U. S. size, how literally tiny were the scores upon scores of men far down below who were doing this thing, its significance regained bit by bit its proper proportions. Train after train–load of the spoil of the "cut" ground away towards the Pacific; and here man had been digging steadily, if not always earnestly, since a year before I was born. The gigantic scene recalled to the mind the "industrial army" of which Carlyle was prone to preach, with the same discipline and organization as an army in the field; and every now and then, to bear out the figure, there burst forth the mighty cannonade, not of war, but of peace and progress in the form of earth–upheaving and house–rocking blasts of dynamite, tearing away the solid rock below at the very feet of the town.

I took to the railroad and struck on further into the unknown country. Almost before I was well started I found myself in another town, yet larger than Culebra and with the name "Empire" in the station building; and nearly every rod of the way between had been lined with villages of negroes and all breeds and colors of canal workers. So on again along a broad macadamized highway that bent and rose through low bushy ridges, past an army encamped in wood and tin barracks on a hillside, with khaki uniformed soldiers ahorse and afoot enlivening all the roadway and the neighboring fields. Never a mile without its town—how different will all this be when the canal is finished and all this community is gone to Alaska or has scattered itself again over the face of the earth, and dense tropical solitude has settled down once more over the scene.

Panama, they had said, is insupportably hot. Comparing it with other lands I knew I could not but smile at the notion. Again it was the lack of perspective. Sweat ran easily, yet so fresh the air and so refreshing the breeze sweeping incessantly across from the Atlantic that even the sweating was almost enjoyable. Hot! Yes, like June on the Canadian border—though not like July. It is hot in St. Louis on an August Sunday, with all the refreshment doors tight closed—to strangers; hot in the cotton–fields of Texas, but with these plutonic corners the heat of the Zone shows little rivalry.

The way led round a cone–shaped hill crowned by another military camp with the Stars and Stripes flapping far above, until I came at last in sight of the renowned Chagres, seven miles above Culebra, to all appearances a meek and harmless little stream spanned by a huge new iron bridge and forbidden to come and play in the unfinished canal by a little dam of earth that a steam— shovel will some day eat up in a few hours. Here, where it ends and the flat country begins, I descended into the "cut," dry and waterless, with a stone—quarry bottom. A sharp climb out on the opposite side and I plunged into rampant jungle, half expecting snake—bites on my exposed ankles—another pre—conceived notion— and at length falling into a narrow jungle trail that pitched down through a dense—grown gully, came upon a fenced compound with several Zone buildings on the banks of the Chagres, down to which sloped a broad green lawn.

Here dwells hale and ruddy "Old Fritz," for long years keeper of the fluviograph that measures and gives warning of the rampages of the Chagres. Fritz will talk to you in almost any tongue you may choose, as he can tell you of adventures in almost any land, all with a captivating accent and in the vocabulary of a man who has lived long among men and nature. Nor are Fritz' opinions those gleaned from other men or the printed page. So we fell to fanning ourselves this January afternoon on the screened and shaded veranda above the Chagres, and "Old Fritz," lighting his pipe, raised his slippered feet to the screen railing and, tossing away the charred remnant of a match, began:—

"Vidout var dere iss no brogress. Ven all der world iss at peace, all der world goes to shleep."

Police headquarters looked all but deserted on Friday morning. There had been "something doing" in Zone criminal annals the night before, and not only "the Captain" but both "the Chief" and the Inspector were "somewhere out along the line." I sat down in the arm—chair against the wall. A half—hour, perhaps, had I read when "Eddie"—I am not entitled, perhaps, to such familiarity, but the solemn title of "chief clerk" is far too stiff and formal for that soul of good—heartedness striving in vain to hide behind a bluff exterior—"Eddie," I say, blew a last cloud of smoke from his lungs to the ceiling, tossed aside the butt of his cigarette, and motioned to me to take the chair beside his desk.

"It's all off!" said a voice within me. For the expression on "Eddie's" face was that of a man with an unpleasant duty to perform, and his opening words were in exactly that tone of voice in which a man begins, "I am sorry, but—" Had I not often used it myself?

"The Captain," is how he really did begin, "called me up from Colon last night, and—"

9

"Here's where I get my case nol prossed," I found myself whispering. In all probability that sealed document I had sent in the day before announced me as a physical wreck.

"—and told me," continued "Eddie" in his sad, regretful tone, "to tell you we will take you on the force as a first–class policeman. It happens, however, that the department of Civil Administration is about to begin a census of the Zone, and they are looking for any men that can speak Spanish. If we take you on, therefore, the Captain would assign you to the census department until that work is done—it will probably take something over a month—and then you would be returned to regular police duty. The Chief says he'd rather have you learn the Isthmus on census than on police pay.

"Or," went on "Eddie," just as I was about to break in with, "All right, that suits me,"—"or, if you prefer, the census department will enroll you as a regular enumerator and we'll take you on the force as soon as that job is over. The—er—pay," added "Eddie," reaching for a cigarette but changing his mind, "of enumerators will be five dollars a day, and—er—five a day beats eighty a month by more than a nose."

We descended a story and I was soon in conference with a slender, sharp–faced young man of mobile features and penetrating eyes behind which a smile seemed always to be lurking. On the Canal Zone, as in British colonies, one is frequently struck by the youthfulness of men in positions of importance.

"I'll probably assign you to Empire district," the slender young man was saying, "there's everything up there and almost any language will sure be some help to us. This time we are taking a thorough, complete census of all the Zone clear back to the Zone line. Here's a sample card and list of instructions."

In other words kind Uncle Sam was about to give me authority to enter every dwelling in the most cosmopolitan and thickly populated district of his Canal Zone, and to put questions to every dweller therein, note–book and pencil in hand; authority to ramble around a month or more in sunshine and jungle—and pay me for the privilege. There are really two methods of seeing the Canal Zone; as an employee or as a guest at the Tivoli, both of them at about five dollars a day—but at opposite ends of the thermometer.

There remained a week–end between that Friday morning and the last day of January, set for the beginning of the census. Certainly I should not regret the arrival of the day when I should become an employee, with all the privileges and coupon–books thereunto appertained. For the Zone is no easy dwelling–place for the non– employee. Our worthy Uncle of the chin whiskers makes it quite plain that, while he may tolerate the mere visitor, he does not care to have him hanging around; makes it so plain, in fact, that a few weeks purely of sight–seeing on the Zone implies an adamantine financial backing. In his screened and full–provided towns, where the employee lives in such well–furnished comfort, the tourist might beat his knuckles bare and shake yellow gold in the other hand, and be coldly refused even a lodging for the night; and while he may eat a meal in the employees' hotels—at near twice the employee's price—the very attitude in which he is received says openly that he is admitted only on suffrance— permitted to eat only because if he starved to death our Uncle would have the bother of burying him and his Zone Police the arduous toil of making out an accident report.

Meanwhile I must change my dwelling–place. For the quartermaster of Corozal had need of all the rooms within his domain, need so imperative that seventeen bona fide and wrathy employees were even then bunking in the pool–room of Corozal hotel. Work on the Zone was moving steadily Pacificward and the accommodations refused to come with it—at least at the same degree of speed.

Nor was I especially averse to the transfer. The room–mate with whom fate had cast me in House 81 was a pleasant enough fellow, a youth of unobjectionable personal manners even though his "eight– hour graft" was in the sooty seat of a steam–crane high above Miraflores locks. But he had one slight idiosyncrasy that might in time have grown annoying. On the night of our first acquaintance, after we had lain exchanging random experiences till the evening heat had begun a retreat before the gentle night breeze, I was awakened from the first doze by my companion sitting suddenly up in his cot across the room.

"Say, I hope you're not nervous?" he remarked.

"Not immoderately."

"One of my stunts is night–mare," he went on, rising to switch on the electric light, "and when I get 'em I generally imagine my room–mate is a burglar trying to go through my junk and—"

11

He reached under his pillow and brought to light a "Colt's" of 45 caliber; then crossing the room he pointed to three large irregular splintered holes in the wall some three or four inches above me, and which I had not already seen simply because I had not chanced to look that way.

"There's the last three. But I'm tryin' to break myself of 'em," he concluded, slipping the revolver back under his pillow and turning off the light again.

Which is among the various reasons why it was without protest that, with "the Captain's" telephoned consent on the ground that I was now virtually on the force, I took up my residence in Corozal police station. 'T is a peaceful little building of the usual Zone type on a breezy knoll across the railroad, with a spreading tree and a little well–tended flower plot before it, and the broad world stretching away in all directions behind. Here lived Policeman T——and B——." First–class policemen" perhaps I should take care to specify, for in Zone parlance the unqualified noun implies African ancestry. But it seems easier to use an adjective of color when necessary. Among their regular duties was that of weighing down the rocking–chairs on the airy front veranda, whence each nook and cranny of Corozal was in sight, and of strolling across to greet the train–guard of the seven daily passengers; though the irregular ones that might burst upon them at any moment were not unlikely to resemble a Moro expedition in the Philippines. B—— and I shared the big main room; for T——, being the haughty station commander, occupied the parlor suite beside the office. That was all, except the black Trinidadian boy who sat on the wooden shelf that was his bed behind a huge padlocked door and gazed dreamily out through the bars—when he was not carrying a bundle to the train for his wardens or engaged in the janitor duties that kept Corozal station so spick and span. Oh! To be sure there were also a couple of negro policemen in the smaller room behind the thin wooden partition of our own, but negro policemen scarcely count in Zone Police reckonings.

"By Heck! They must use a lot o' mules t' haul aout all thet dirt," observed an Arkansas farmer to his nephew, home from the Zone on vacation. He would have thought so indeed could he have spent a day at Corozal and watched the unbroken deafening procession of dirt–trains scream by on their way to the Pacific,— straining Moguls dragging a furlong of "Lidgerwood flats," swaying "Oliver dumps" with their side chains clanking, a succession as incessant of "empties" grinding back again into the midst of the fray. On the tail of every train lounged an American conductor, dressed more like a miner, though his "front" and "hind" negro brakemen were as apt to be in silk ties and patent–leathers.

To say nothing of the train-loads that go Atlanticward and to jungle "dumps" and to many an unnoticed "fill." Then when he had thus watched the day through it would have been of interest to go and chat with some of the "Old Timers" who live here beside the track and who have seen, or at least heard, this same endless stream of rock and earth race by six days a week, fifty-two weeks a year for six years, as constant and heavily-laden to-day as in the beginning. He might discover, as not all his fellow-countrymen have as yet, that the little surgical operation on Mother Earth we are engaged in is no mule job.

The week-end gave me time to get back in touch with affairs in the States among the newspaper files at the Y. M. C. A. building. Uncle Sam surely makes life comfortable for his children wherever he takes hold. It is not enough that he shall clean up and set in order these tropical pest-holes; he will have the employee fancy himself completely at home. Here I sat in one of the dozen big airy recreation halls, well stocked with man's playthings, which the government has erected on the Zone; I, who two weeks before had been thankful for lodging on the earth floor of a Honduranean hut. The Y. M. C. A. is the chief social center on the Isthmus, the rendezvous and leisure-hour headquarters of the thousands that inhabit bachelor quarters—except the few of the purely barroom type. "Everybody's Association" it might perhaps more properly be called, for ladies find welcome and the laughter of children over the parlor games is rarely lacking. It is not the circumspect place that are many of its type in the States, but a real man's place where he can buy his cigarettes and smoke his pipe in peace, a place for men as men are, not as the fashion plates that mama's fond imagination pictures them. With all its excellences it would be unjust to complain that the Zone "Y. M." is a trifle "low-brow" in its tastes, that the books on its shelves are apt to be "popular" novels rather than reading matter, that its phonographs are most frequently screeching vaudeville noises while the Slezak and Homer disks lie tucked away far down near the bottom of the stack.

With the new week I moved to Empire, the "Rules and Regulations" in a pocket and the most indispensable of my possessions under an arm. Once more we rumbled through Miraflores tunnel through a mole-hill, past her concrete light-house among the astonished palms, and her giant hose of water wiping away the rock hills, across the trestleless bridge with its photographic glimpse of the canal before and behind for the limber-necked, and again I found myself in the metropolis of the Canal Zone. At the quartermaster's office my "application for quarters" was duly filed without a word and a slip assigning me to Room 3, House 47, as silently returned. I climbed by a stone-faced

13

U. S. road to my new home on the slope of a ridge overlooking the railway and its buildings below.

It was the noon–hour. My two room–mates, therefore, were on hand for inspection, sprawlingly engrossed in a—quite innocent and legal—card game on a table littered with tobacco, pipes, matches, dog–eared wads of every species of literature from real estate pamphlets to locomotive journals, and a further mass of indiscriminate matter that none but a professional inventory man would attempt to classify. About the room was the usual clutter of all manner of things in the usual unarranged, "unwomaned" Zone way, which the negro janitor feels it neither his duty nor privilege to bring to order; while on and about my cot and bureau were helter–skeltered the sundry possessions of an absent employee, who had left for his six–weeks' vacation without hanging up his shirt—after the fashion of "Zoners." So when I had wiped away the dust that had been gathering thereon since the days of de Lesseps and chucked my odds and ends into a bureau drawer, I was settled,—a full–fledged Zone employee in the quarters to which every man on the "gold roll" is entitled free of charge.

Just here it may be well to explain that the I. C. C. has very dexterously dodged the necessity of lining the Zone with the offensive signs "Black" and "White." 'T would not be exactly the distinction desired anyway. Hence the line has been drawn between "Gold" and "Silver" employees. The first division, paid in gold coin, is made up, with a few exceptions, of white American citizens. To the second belong any of the darker shade, and all common laborers of whatever color, these receiving their wages in Panamanian silver. 'T is a deep and sharp–drawn line. The story runs that Liza Lawsome, not long arrived from Jamaica, entering the office of a Zone dentist, paused suddenly before the announcement:

Crownwork. Gold and Silver Fillings.
Extractions wholly without Pain.

There was deep disappointment in face and voice as she sat down with a flounce of her starched and snow–white skirt, gasping:

"Oh, Doctah, does I HAVE to have silver fillings?"

14

My room—mates, "Mitch" and "Tom," sat respectively at the throttle of a locomotive that jerked dirt—trains out of the "cut" and straddled a steam—shovel that ate its way into Culebra range. Whence, of course, they were covered with the grease and grime incident to those occupations. Which did not make them any the less companionable—though it did promise a distinct increase in my laundry bill. When they had descended again to the labor—train and been snatched away to their appointed tasks, I sat a short hour in one of the black "Mission" rocking—chairs on the screened veranda puzzling over a serious problem. The quarters of the "gold" employee is as completely furnished as any reasonable man could demand, his iron cot with springs and mattress unimpeachable—but just there the maternal generosity of the government ceases. He must furnish his own sheets and pillow—MUST because placards on the wall sternly warn him not to sleep on the bare mattress; and the New York Sunday edition that had served me thus far I had carelessly left behind at Corozal police station. To be sure there were sheets for sale in Empire, at the Commissary—where money has the purchasing—power of cobble—stones, and coupon—books come only to those who have worked a day or more on the Zone. Then the Jamaican janitor, drifting in to potter about the room, evidently guessed the cause of my perplexity, for he turned to point to the bed of the absent "Mitch" and gurgled:

"Jes' you make lub to dat man what got dat bed. Him got plenty ob sheets." Which proved a wise suggestion.

Empire hotel sat a bit down the hill. There the "gold" ranks were again subdivided. The coatless ate and sweltered inside the great dining—room; the formal sat in haughty state in what was virtually a second—story veranda overlooking the railroad yards and a part of the town, where were tables of four, electric fans, and "Ben" to serve with butler formality. I found it worth while to climb the hill for my coat thrice a day. As yet I was jangling down a Panamanian dollar at each appearance, but the day was not far distant when I should receive the "recruits" hotel—book and soon grow as accustomed as the rest to having a coupon snatched from it by the yellow negro at the door. Uncle Sam's boarding scale on the Zone is widely varied. Three meals cost the non—employee $1.50, the "gold" employee $.90, the white European laborer $.40, and negroes in general $.30.

That afternoon, when the sun had begun to bow its head on the thither side of the canal, I climbed to the newly labeled census office on the knoll behind the police station, from the piazza of which all native Empire lies within sweep of the eye. "The boss," a smiling youth only well started on his third decade, whose regular duties were in the sanitary department, had already moved bed, bag, and baggage into the room that had been assigned the census, that he might be "always on the job."

Not till eight that evening, however, did the force gather to look itself over. There was the commander–in–chief of the census bureau, sent down from Washington specifically for the task in hand, under whom as chairmen we settled down into a sort of director's meeting, a wholly informal, coatless, cigarette–smoking meeting in which even the chief himself did not feel it necessary to let his dignity weigh upon him. He had been sent down alone. Hence there had been great scrambling to gather together on the Zone men enough who spoke Spanish—and with no striking success. Most noticeable of my fellow–enumerators, being in uniform, were three Marines from Bas Obispo, fluent with the working Spanish they had picked up from Mindanao to Puerto Rico, and flush–cheeked with the prospect of a full month on "pass," to say nothing of the $4.40 a day that would be added to their daily military income of $.60. Then there were four of darker hue,—Panamanians and West Indians; and how rare are Spanish–speaking, Americans on the Zone was proved by the admittance of such complexions to the "gold" roll.

Of native U. S. civilians there were but two of us. Of whom Barter, speaking only his nasal New Jersey, must perforce be assigned to the "gold" quarters, leaving me the native town of Empire. At which we were both satisfied, Barter because he did not like to sully himself by contact with foreigners, I because one need not travel clear to the Canal Zone to study the ways of Americans. As for the other seven, each was assigned his strip of land something over a mile wide and five long running back to the western boundary of the Zone. That region of wilderness known as "Beyond the Canal" was to be left for special treatment later. The Zone had been divided for census purposes into four sections, with headquarters and supervisor in Ancon, Empire, Gorgona, and Cristobal respectively. Our district, stretching from the trestleless bridge over the canal to a great tree near Bas Obispo, was easily the fat of the land, the most populous, most cosmopolitan, and embracing within its limits the greatest task on the Zone.

Meanwhile we had fallen to studying the "Instructions to Enumerators," the very first article of which was such as to give pause and reflection;

"When you have once signed on as an enumerator you cannot cease to exercise your functions as such without justifiable cause under penalty of $500 fine." Which warning was quickly followed by the hair–raising announcement:

"If you set down the name of a fictitious person"—what can have given the good census department the notion of such a possibility?—"you will be fined $2,000 or sentenced to five years' imprisonment, or both."

From there on the injunctions grew less nerve–racking: "You must use a medium soft black pencil (which will be furnished)"—law– breaking under such conditions would be absurdity—"use no ditto marks and"—here I could not but shudder as there passed before my eyes memories of college lecture rooms and all the strange marks that have come to mean something to me alone—" take pains to write legibly!"

Then we arose and swarmed upstairs to an empty court–room, where Judge G——, throwing away his cigarette and removing his Iowa feet from the bar of justice, caused us each to raise a right hand and swear an oath as solemn as ever president on March fourth. An oath, I repeat, not merely to uphold and defend the constitution against all enemies, armed or armless, but furthermore "not to share with any one any of the information you gather as an enumerator, or show a census card, or keep a copy of same." Yet, I trust I can spin this simple yarn of my Canal Zone days without offense to Uncle Sam against the day when mayhap I shall have occasion to apply to him again for occupation. For that reason I shall take abundant care to give no information whatsoever in the following pages.

CHAPTER II

"The boss" and I initiated the Canal Zone Census that very night. Legally it was to begin with the dawning of February, but there were many labor camps in our district and the hours bordering on midnight the only sure time to "catch 'em in." Up in House 47 I gathered together the legion paraphernalia of this new occupation,—some two hundred red cards a foot long and half as wide, a surveyor's field notebook for the preservation of miscellaneous information, tags for the tagging of canvassed buildings, tacks for the tacking of the same, the necessary tack– hammer, the medium soft black pencil, above all the awesome legal "Commission," impressively signed and sealed, wherein none other than our weighty nation's chief himself did expressly authorize me to search out, enter, and question ad libitum. All this swung over a shoulder in a white canvas sack, that carried memory back through the long years to my newsboy days, I descended to the town.

"The boss" was ready. It was nearly eleven when we crossed the silent P. R. R. tracks and, plunging away into the night past great heaps of abandoned locomotives huddled dim and uncertain in the thin moonlight like ghosts of the French fiasco, dashed into a camp of the laborer's village of Cunette, pitched on the very edge of the now black and silent void of the canal. Eighteen thick– necked negroes in undershirts and trousers gazed up white–eyed from a suspended card game at the long camp table. But we had no time for explanations.

"Name?" I shouted at the coal–hued Hercules nearest at hand.

"David Providence," he bleated in trembling voice, and the great Zone questionnaire was on.

We had enrolled the group before a son of wisdom among them surmised that we were not, after all, plain–clothes men in quest of criminals; and his announcement brought visible relief. Twice as many blacks were sprawled in the two rows of double–sided, three–story bunks,—mere strips of canvas on gas–pipes that could be hung up like swinging shelves when not in use. Mere noise did not even disturb their dreams. We roused them by pencil–jabs in the ribs, and they started up with savage, animal–like grunts and murderous glares which instantly subsided to sheepish grins and voiceless astonishment at sight of a white face bending over them. Now and again open–mouthed guffaws of laughter greeted the mumbled admission of some powerful buck that he could not read, or did not know his age. But there was nothing even faintly resembling insolence, for these were all British West Indians without a corrupting "States nigger" among them. A half–hour after our arrival we had tagged the barracks and dived into the next camp, blacker and sleepier and more populous than the first. It was February morning before I climbed the steps of silent 47 and stepped under the shower–bath that is always preliminary, on the Zone, to a night's repose.

A dream of earthquake, holocaust, and general destruction developed gradually into full consciousness at four–thirty. House 47 was in riotous uproar. No, neither conflagration nor foreign invasion was pending; it was merely the houseful of engineers in their customary daily struggle to catch the labor–train and be away to work by daylight. When the hour's rampage had subsided I rose to switch off the light and turned in again.

The rays of the impetuous Panama sun were spattering from them when I passed again the jumbled rows of invalided locomotives and machinery, reddish with rust and bound, like Gulliver, by green jungle strands and tropical creepers. By day the arch–roofed labor–camps were silent and empty, but for a lonely janitor languidly mopping a floor. Before the buildings a black gang was dipping the canvas and gas–pipe bunks one by one into a great kettle of scalding water. But there are also "married quarters" at Cunette. A row of six government houses tops the ridge, with six families in each house, and—no, I dare not risk nomination to an ever expanding though unpopular club by stating how many in a family. I will venture merely to assert that when noon–time came I was not well started on the second house, yet carried away more than sixty filled–out cards.

More than two days that single row of houses endured, varied by nights spent with "the boss" in the labor–camps of Lirio, Culebra way. Then one morning I tramped far out the highway to the old Scotchman's farm–house that bounds Empire on the north and began the long intricate journey through the private–owned town itself. It was like attending a congress of the nations, a museum exhibition of all the shapes and hues in which the human vegetable grows. Tenements and wobbly–kneed shanties swarming with exhibits monopolized the landscape; strange the room that did not yield up at least a man and woman and three or four children. Day after blazing day I sat on rickety chairs, wash–tubs, ironing–boards, veranda railings, climbing creaking stairways, now and again descending a treacherous one in unintentional haste and ungraceful posture, burrowing into blind but inhabited cubby–holes, hunting out squatters' nests of tin cans and dry–goods boxes hidden away behind the legitimate buildings, shouting questions into dilapidated ear–drums, delving into the past of every human being who fell in my way. West Indian negroes easily kept the lead of all other nationalities combined; negroes blacker than the obsidian cutlery of the Aztecs, blonde negroes with yellow hair and blue eyes whose race was betrayed only by eyelids and the dead whiteness of skin, and whom one could not set down as such after enrolling swarthy Spaniards as "white" without a smile.

They lived chiefly in windowless, six–by–eight rooms, always a cheap, dirty calico curtain dividing the three–foot parlor in front from the five–foot bedroom behind, the former cluttered with a van–load of useless junk, dirty blankets, decrepit furniture, glittering gewgaws, a black baby squirming naked in a basket of rags with an Episcopal prayerbook under its pillow—relic of the old demon–scaring superstitions of Voodoo worship. Every inch of the walls was "decorated," after the artistic temperament of the race, with pages of illustrated magazines or newspapers, half– tones of all things conceivable with no small amount of text in sundry languages, many a page purely of advertising matter, the muscular, imbruted likeness of a certain black champion rarely missing, frequently with a Bible laid reverently beneath it. Outside, before each room, a tin fireplace for cooking precariously bestrided the veranda rail.

Often a tumble–down hovel where three would seem a crowd yielded up more than a dozen inmates, many of whom, being at work, must be looked for later—the "back–calls" that is the bete–noire of the census enumerator. West Indians, however, are for the most part well acquainted with the affairs of friends and room–mates, and enrolment of the absent was often possible. Occasionally I ran into a den of impertinence that must be frowned down, notably a notorious swarming tenement over a lumber–yard. But on the whole the courtesy of British West Indians, even among themselves, was noteworthy. Of the two great divisions among them, Barbadians seemed more well–mannered than Jamaicans—or was it merely more subtle hypocrisy? Among them all the most unspoiled children of nature appeared to be those from the little island of Nevis.

"You ain't no American?"

"Yes, ah is."

"Why, you de bery furst American ah eber see dat was perlite."

Which spoke badly indeed for the others, that not being one of the virtues I strive particularly to cultivate.

But "perlite" or not, there can be no question of the astounding stupidity of the West Indian rank and file, a stupidity amusing if you are in an amusable mood, unendurable if you neglect to pack your patience among your bag of supplies in the morning. Tropical patience, too, is at best a frail child. The dry–season sun rarely even veiled his face, and there were those among the enumerators who complained of the taxing labor of all–day marching up and down streets and stairs and Zone hills beneath it; but to me, fresh from tramping over the mountains of Central America with twenty pounds on my shoulders, this was mere pastime. Heat had no terrors for the enumerated, however. Often in the hottest hour of the day I came upon negroes sleeping in tightly closed rooms, the sweat running off them in streams, yet apparently vastly enjoying the situation.

Sunday came and I chose to continue, though virtually all the Zone was on holiday and even "the boss," after what I found later to be his invariable custom, had broken away from his card–littered dwelling–place on Saturday evening and hurried away to Panama, drawn thither and held till Monday morning—by some irresistible attraction. Sunday turns holiday completely on the Zone, even to hours of trains and hotels. The frequent passengers were packed from southern white end to northern black end with all nations in gladsome garb, bound Panamaward to see the lottery drawing and buy a ticket for the following Sunday, across the Isthmus to breezy Colon, or to one of a hundred varying spots and pastimes. Others in khaki breeches fresh from the government laundry in Cristobal and the ubiquitous leather leggings of the "Zoner" were off to ride out the day in the jungles; still others set resolutely forth afoot into tropical paths; a dozen or so, gleaned one by one from all the towns along the line were even on their way to church. Yet with all this scattering there still remained a respectable percentage lounging on the screened verandas in pajamas and kimonas, "Old Timers" of four or five or even six years' standing who were convinced they had seen and heard, and smelt and tasted all that the Zone or tropical lands have to offer.

Well on in the morning there was a general gathering of all the ditch–digging clans of Empire and vicinity in a broad field close under the eaves of the town, and soon there came drifting across to me at my labor, hoarse, frenzied screams; sounding strangely incongruous beneath the swaying palm–trees;

"Come on! Get down with his arm! Aaaaahrrr!"

But my time was well chosen. In the Spanish camps above the canal, still and silent with Sunday, men at no other time to be run to earth were entrapped in their bunks, under their dwelling–places in the shade, shaving, exchanging hair–cuts, washing workaday clothes, reminiscing over far–off homes and pre–migratory days, or merely loafing. The same cheery, friendly, quick–witted fellows they were as in their native land, even the few Italians and rare Portuguese scattered among them inoculated with their cheerfulness.

21

Came sudden changes to camps of Martiniques, a sort of wild, untamed creature, who spoke a distressing imitation of French which even he did not for a moment claim to be such, but frankly dubbed patois. Restless-eyed black men who answered to their names only at the question "Cummun t'appelle?" and give their age only to those who open wide their mouths and cry, "Caje-vous?" Then on again to the no less strange, sing-song "English" of Jamaica, the whining tones of those whose island trees the conquesting Spaniards found bearded—"barbados"—now and again a more or less dark Costa Rican, Guatemalteco, Venezuelan, stray islanders from St. Vincent, Trinidad, or Guadalupe, individuals defying classification. But the chief reward for denying myself a holiday were the "back-calls" in the town itself which I was able to check out of my field-book. Many a long-sought negro I roused from his holiday siesta, dashing past the tawdry calico curtains to pound him awake—mere auricular demonstration having only the effect of lulling him into deeper child-like slumber. The surest and often only effective means was to tickle the slumberer gently on the soles of the bare feet with some airy, delicate instrument such as my tack-hammer, or a convenient broom-handle or flat-iron. Frequently I came upon young negro men of the age and type that in white skins would have been loafing on pool-room corners, reading to themselves in loud and solemn voices from the Bible, with a far-away look in their eyes; always I was surrounded by a never- broken babble of voices, for the West Indian negro can let his face run unceasingly all the day through, and the night, though he have never a word to say.

Thus my "enumerated" tags spread further and wider over the city of Empire. I reached in due time the hodge-podge shops and stores of Railroad Avenue. Chinamen began to drift into the rolls, there appeared such names as Carmen Wah Chang, cooks and waitresses living in darksome back cupboards must be unearthed, negro shoemakers were caught at their stands on the sidewalks, shiny- haired bartenders gave up their biographies in nasal monosyllables amid the slop of "suds" and the scrape of celluloid froth- eradicators. Rare was the land that had not sent representatives to this great dirt-shoveling congress. A Syrian merchant gasped for breath and fell over his counter in delight to find that I, too, had been in his native Zakleh, five Punjabis all but died of pleasure when I mispronounced three words of their tongue. Occasionally there came startling contrast as I burst unexpectedly into the ancestral home of some educated native family that had withstood all the tides of time and change and still lived in the beloved "Emperador" of their forefathers. Anger was usually near the surface at my intrusion, but they quickly changed to their ingrown politeness and chatty sociability when addressed in their own tongue and treated in their own extravagant gestures. It was almost sure to return again, however, at the question whether they were Panamanians. Distinctly not! They were Colombians! There is no such country as Panama.

Thus the enrolling of the faithful continued. Chinese laundrymen divulged the secrets of their mysterious past between spurts of water at steaming shirt–bosoms; Chinese merchants, of whom there are hordes on the Zone, cueless, dressed and betailored till you must look at them twice to tell them from "gold" employees, the flag of the new republic flapping above their doors, the new president in their lapels, left off selling crucifixes and breastpin medallions of Christ to negro women, to answer my questions. One evening I stumbled into a nest of eleven Bengali peddlers with the bare floor of their single room as bed, table, and chairs; in one corner, surmounted by their little embroidered skull–caps, were stacked the bundles with which they pester Zone housewives, and in another their god wrapped in a dirty rag against profaning eyes.

Many days had passed before I landed the first Zone resident I could not enroll unassisted. He was a heathen Chinee newly arrived, who spoke neither Spanish nor English. It was "Chinese Charlie" who helped me out. "Chinese Charlie" was a resident of the Zone before the days of de Lesseps and at our first meeting had insisted on being enrolled under that pseudonym, alleging it his real name. Upstairs above his store all was sepulchral silence when I mounted to investigate—and I came quickly and quietly down again; for the door had opened on the gaudy Oriental splendor of a joss–house where dwelt only grinning wooden idols not counted as Zone residents by the materialistic census officials. On the Isthmus as elsewhere "John" is a law–abiding citizen—within limits; never obsequious, nearly always friendly, ready to answer questions quite cheerily so long as he considers the matter any of your business, but closing infinitely tighter than the maltreated bivalve when he fancies you are prying too far.

In time I reached the Commissary—the government department store —and enrolled it from cash–desk to cold–storage; Empire hotel, from steward to scullions, filed by me whispering autobiography; the police station on its knoll fell like the rest. I went to jail—and set down a large score of black men and a pair of European whites, back from a day's sweaty labor of road building, who lived now in unaccustomed cleanliness in the heart of the lower story of a fresh wooden building with light iron bars, easy to break out of were it not that policemen, white and black, sleep on all sides of them. Crowded old Empire not only faces her streets but even her back yards are filled with shacks and inhabited boxes to be hunted out. On the hem of her tattered outskirts and the jungle edges I ran into heaps of old abandoned junk,—locomotives, cars, dredges, boilers (some with the letters "U. S." painted upon them, which sight gave some three–day investigator material to charge the I. C. C. with untold waste); all now soon to be removed by a Chicago wrecking company.

Then all the town must be done again—"back calls." By this time so wide and varied was my acquaintance in Empire that wenches withdrew a dripping hand from their tubs to wave at me with a sympathetic giggle, and piccaninnies ran out to meet me as I returned in quest of one missing inmate in a house of fifty. For the few laborers still uncaught I took to coming after dark. But West Indians rarely own lamps, not even the brass tax–numbers above the doors were visible, and as for a negro in the dark—

Absurd rumors had begun early to circulate among the darker brethren. In all negrodom the conviction became general that this individual detailed catechising and house–branding was really a government scheme to get lists of persons due for deportation, either for lack of work as the canal neared completion or for looseness of marital relations. Hardly a tenement did I enter but laughing voices bandied back and forth and there echoed and reechoed through the building such remarks as:

"Well, dey gon' sen' us home, Penelope," or "Yo an' Percival better hurry up an' git married, Ambrosia."

Several dusky females regularly ran away whenever I approached; one at least I came a–seeking in vain nine times, and found her the tenth behind a garbage barrel. Many fancied the secret marks on the "enumerated" tag—date, and initials of the enumerator— were intimately concerned with their fate. So strong is the fear of the law imbued by the Zone Police that they dared not tear down the dreaded placard, but would sometimes sit staring at it for hours striving to penetrate its secret or exorcise away its power of evil, and now and then some bolder spirit ventured out—at midnight—with a pencil and put tails and extra flourishes on the penciled letters in the hope of disguising them against the fatal day.

Except for the chaos of nationalities and types on the Zone, enumerating would have become more than monotonous. But the enumerated took care to break the monotony. There was the wealth of nomenclature for instance. What more striking than a shining–black waiter strutting proudly about under the name of Levi McCarthy? There was no necessity of asking Beresford Plantaganet if he were a British subject. Naturally the mother of Hazarmaneth Cumberbath Smith, baptized that very week, had to claw out the family Bible from among the bed–clothes and look up the name on the fly–leaf.

To the enumerator, who must set down concise and exact answers to each of his questions, fifty or sixty daily scenes and replies something like these were delightful;

Enumerator (sitting down on the edge of a barrel): "How many living in this room?"

Explosive laughter from the buxom, jet–black woman addressed.

Enumerator (on a venture): "What's the man's name?"

"He name 'Rasmus Iggleston."

"What's his metal–check number?"

"Lard, mahster, ah don' know he check number."

"Haven't you a commissary–book with it in?"

"Lard no, mah love, commissary–book him feeneesh already befo' las' week."

"Is he a Jamaican?"

"No, him a Mont–rat, mahster." (Monsterratian.)

"What color is he?"

"Te! He! Wha' fo' yo as' all dem questions, mahster?"

"For instance."

"Oh, him jes' a pitch darker'n me."

"How old is he?"

(Loud laughter) "Law', ah don' know how ol' him are!"

"Well, about how old?"

"Oh, him a ripe man, mah love, him a prime man."

"Is he older than you?"

"Oh, yes, him older 'n me."

"And how old are you?"

"Te! He! 'Deed ah don' know how ol' ah is; ah gone los' mah age paper."

"Is he married?"

(Quickly and with very grave face) "Oh, yes indeed, mahster, Ah his sure 'nough wife."

"Can he read?"

(Hesitatingly) "Er—a leetle, sir, not too much, sir." (Which generally means he can spell out a few words of one syllable and make some sort of mark representing his name.)

"What kind of work does he do?"

(Haughtily) "Him employed by de I. C. C."

"Yes, naturally. But what kind of work does he do. Is he a laborer?"

(Quickly and very impressively) "Laborer! Oh, no, mah sweet mahster, he jes' shovel away de dirt befo' de steam shovel."

"All right. That 'll do for 'Rasmus. Now your name?"

"Mah name Mistress Jane Iggleston."

"How long have you lived on the Canal Zone?"

"Oh, not too long, mah love."

"Since when have you lived in this house?"

"Oh, we don' come to dis house too long, sah."

"Can you read and write?"

"No, ah don' stay in Jamaica. Ah come to Panama when ah small."

"Do you do any work besides your own housework?"

(Evasively) "Work? If ah does any work? No, not any."

Enumerator looks hard from her to washtub.

"Ah—er—oh, ah washes a couple o' gentlemen's clot'es."

"Very good. Now then, how many children?"

"We don' git no children, sah."

"What! How did that happen?"

Loud, house–shaking laughter.

Enumerator (looking at watch and finding it 12:10): "Well, good afternoon."

"Good evenin', sah. Thank you, sah. Te! He!"

Variations on the above might fill many pages:

"How old are you?"

Self—appointed interpreter of the same shade; "He as' how old is yo?"

"How old *I* are? Ah don rightly know mah age, mahster, mah mother never tol' me."

St. Lucian woman, evidently about forty—five, after deep thought, plainly anxious to be as truthful as possible: "Er—ah's twenty, sir."

"Oh, you're older than that. About sixty, say?"

"'Bout dat, sah."

"Are you married?"

(Pushing the children out of the way.) "N—not as yet, mah sweet mahster, bu—but—but we go 'n' be soon, sah."

To a Barbadian woman of forty: "Just you and your daughter live here?"

"Dat's all, sir."

"Doesn't your husband live here?"

"Oh, ah don't never marry as yet, sah."

Anent the old saying about the partnership of life and hope.

To a Dominican woman of fifty—two, toothless and pitted with small—pox: "Are you married?"

(With simpering smile) "Not as yet, mah sweet mahster."

To a Jamaican youth;

"How many people live in this room?"

"Three persons live here, sir."

"I stand grammatically corrected. When did you move here?"

"We remove here in April."

"Again I apologize for my mere American grammar. Now, Henry, what is your room−mate's name?"

"Well, we calls him Ethel, but I don't know his right title. Peradventure he will not work this evening [afternoon] and you can ask him from himself."

"Do his parents live on the Zone?"

"Oh, yes, sah, he has one father and one mother."

An answer: "Why HIMSELF [emphatic subject pronoun among Barbadians] didn't know if he'd get a job."

To a six−foot black giant working as night−hostler of steam− shovels:

"Well, Josiah, I suppose you're a Jamaican?"

"Oh, yes, boss, ah work in Kingston ten years as a bar−maid."

"Married?"

"No, boss, ah's not 'xactly married. Ah's livin' with a person."

A colored family:

Sarah Green, very black, has a child named Edward White, and is now living with Henry Brown, a light yellow negro.

West Indian wit:

A shop−sign in Empire: "Don't ask for credit. He is gone on vacation since January 1, 1912."

Laughter and carefree countenances are legion in the West Indian ranks, children seem never to be punished, and to all appearances man and wife live commonly in peace and harmony. Dr. O——tells the following story, however:

In his rounds he came upon a negro beating his wife and had him placed under arrest. The negro: "Why, boss, can't a man chastize his wife when she desarves and needs it?"

Dr. O——: "Not on the Canal Zone. It's against the law."

Negro (in great astonishment): "Is dat so, boss. Den ah'll never do it again, boss—on de Canal Zone."

One morning in the heart of Empire a noise not unlike that of a rocky waterfall began to grow upon my ear. Louder and louder it swelled as I worked slowly forward. At last I discovered its source. In a lower room of a tenement an old white–haired Jamaican had fitted up a private school, to which the elite among the darker brethren sent their children, rather than patronize the common public schools Uncle Sam provides free to all Zone residents. The old man sat before some twenty wide–eyed children, one of whom stood slouch–shouldered, book in hand, in the center of the room, and at regular intervals of not more than twenty seconds he shouted high above all other noises of the neighborhood:

"Yo calls dat Eng–leesh! How eber yo gon' l'arn talk proper lika dat, yo tell me?"

Far back in the interior of an Empire block I came upon an old, old negro woman, parchment–skinned and doddering, living alone in a stoop–shouldered shanty of boxes and tin cans. "Ah don' know how ol' ah is, mahster," was one of her replies, "but ah born six years befo' de cholera diskivered."

"When did you come to Panama?"

"Ah don' know, but it a long time ago."

"Before the Americans, perhaps?"

"Oh, long befo'! De French ain't only jes' begin to dig. Ah's ashamed to say how long ah been here" (just why was not evident, unless she fancied she should long ago have made her fortune and left). "Is you a American? Well, de Americans sure have done one thing. Dey mak' dis country civilize. Why, chil', befo' dey come we have all de time here revolutions. Ah couldn't count to how many revolutions we had, an' ebery time dey steal all what we have. Dey even steal mah clothes. Ah sure glad fo' one de Americans come."

It was during my Empire enumerating that I was startled one morning to burst suddenly from the tawdry, junk–jumbled rooms of negroes into a bare–floored, freshly scrubbed room containing some very clean cots, a small table and a hammock, and a general air of frankness and simplicity, with no attempt to disguise the commonplace. At the table sat a Spaniard in worn but newly washed working–clothes, book in hand. I sat down and, falling unconsciously into the "th" pronunciation of the Castilian, began blithely to reel off the questions that had grown so automatic.

"Name?"–;–Federico Malero. "Check Number?"—"Can you read?" "A little." The barest suggestion of amusement in his voice caused me to look up quickly. "My library," he said, with the ghost of a weird smile, nodding his head slightly toward an unpainted shelf made of pieces of dynamite boxes, "Mine and my room–mates." The shelf was filled with four—REAL Barcelona paper editions of Hegel, Fichte, Spencer, Huxley, and a half–dozen others accustomed to sit in the same company, all dog–eared with much reading.

"Some ambitious foreman," I mused, and went on with my queries:

"Occupation?"

"Pico y pala," he answered.

"Pick and shovel!" I exclaimed—"and read those?"

"No importa," he answered, again with that elusive shadow of a smile, "It doesn't matter," and as I rose to leave, "Buenos dias, senor," and he turned again to his reading.

I plunged into the jumble of negroes next door, putting my questions and setting down the answers without even hearing them, my thoughts still back in the clean, bare room behind, wondering whether I should not have been wiser after all to have ignored the sharp–drawn lines and the prejudices of my fellow–countrymen and joined the pick and shovel Zone world. There might have been pay dirt there. A few months before, I remembered, a Spanish laborer killed in a dynamite explosion in the "cut" had turned out to be one of Spain's most celebrated lawyers. I recalled that EL UNICO, the anarchist Spanish weekly published in Miraflores contains some crystal–clear thinking set forth in a sharp–cut manner that shows a real inside knowledge of the "job" and the canal workers, however little one may agree with its philosophy and methods.

Then it was due to the law of contrasts, I suppose, that the thought of "Tom," my room–mate, suddenly flashed upon me; and I discovered myself chuckling at the picture, "Tom, the Rough–neck," to whom all such as Federico Malero with his pick and shovel were mere "silver men," on whom "Tom" looked down from his high perch on his steam–shovel as far less worthy of notice than the rock he was clawing out of the hillside. How many a silent chuckle and how many a covert sneer must the Maleros on the Zone indulge in at the pompous airs of some American ostensibly far above them.

CHAPTER III

Meanwhile my fellow enumerators were reporting troubles "in the bush." I heard particularly those of two of the Marines, "Mac" and Renson, merry, good–natured, earnest–by–spurts, even modest fellows quite different from what I had hitherto pictured as an enlisted man.

"Mac" was a half and half of Scotch and Italian. Naturally he was constantly effervescing, both verbally and temperamentally, his snapping black eyes were never still, life played across his excitable, sunny boyish face like cloud shadows on a mountain landscape, whoever would speak to him at any length must catch him in a vice–like grip and hold his attention by main force. He spoke with a funny little almost–foreign accent, was touching on forty, and was the youngest man at that age in the length and breadth of the Canal Zone.

At first sight you would take "Mac" for a mere roustabout, like most who go a'soldiering. But before long you'd begin to wonder where he got his rich and fluent vocabulary and his warehouse of information. Then you'd run across the fact that he had once finished a course in a middle–western university—and forgotten it. The schools had left little of their blighting mark upon him, yet "pump" "Mac" on any subject from rapid–fire guns to grand opera and you'd get at least a reasonable answer. Though you wouldn't guess the knowledge was there unless you did pump for it, for "Mac" was not of the type of those who overwork the first person pronoun, not because of foolish diffidence but merely because it rarely occurred to him as a subject of conversation. Seventeen years in the marine corps—you were sure he was "jollying" when he first said it—had taken "Mac" to most places where warships go, from Pekin and "the Islands" to Cape Town and Buenos Ayres, and given him not merely an acquaintance with the world but—what is far more of an acquisition—the gift of getting acquainted in almost any stratum of the world in the briefest possible space of time.

"Mac" spoke not only his English and Italian but a fluent "Islands" Spanish; he knew enough French to talk even to Martiniques, and he could moreover make two distinct sets of noises that were understood by Chinese and Japanese respectively. He was a man just reckless enough in all things to be generous and alive, yet never foolishly wasteful either of himself or his meager substance. "Mac" first rose to fame in the census department by appearing one afternoon at Empire police station dragging a "bush" native by the scruff of the neck with one hand, and carrying in the other the machete with which the bushman had tried to prove he was a Colombian and not subject to questioning by the agents of other powers.

Renson—well, Renson was in some ways "Mac's" exact antithesis and in some his twin brother. He was one of those youths who believe in spending prodigally and in all possible haste what little nature has given them. Wherefore, though he was younger than "Mac" appeared to be, he already looked older than "Mac" was. In Zone parlance "he had already laid a good share of the road to Hell behind him." Yet such a cheery, likable chap was Renson, so large– hearted and unassuming—that was just why you felt an itching to seize him by the collar of his olive–drab shirt and shake him till his teeth rattled for tossing himself so wantonly to the infernal bow–wows.

Renson's "bush" troubles were legion. Not only were there the seducing brown "Spigoty" women out in the wilderness to help him on his descending trail, but when and wherever fire–water of whatever nationality or degree of voltage showed its neck—and it is to be found even in "the bush"—there was Renson sure to give battle—and fall. "It's no use bein' a man unless you're a hell of a man," was Renson's "influenced" philosophy. How different this was from his native good sense when the influence was turned off was demonstrated when he returned from cautiously reconnoitering a cottage far back in the wilds one dark night and reported as his reason for postponing the enumerating: "If you'd butt in on one o' them Martinique booze festivals they'd crown you with a bottle."

Already one or two enumerators had gone back to private life—by request. Particularly sad was the case of our dainty, blue–blooded Panamanian. As with many Panamanians, and not a few of the self– exalted elsewhere, he was more burdened with blue corpuscles than with gray matter. At any rate—

On our cards, after the query "Color?" was a small space, a very small space in which was to be written quite briefly and unceremoniously "W," "B," or "Mx" as the case might be. Uncle Sam was in a hurry for his census. Early one afternoon our Panamanian helpmate burst upon one of his numerous aristocratic relatives in his royal thatched domains in the ancestral bush. When he had embraced him the customary fifteen times on the right side and the fifteen accustomed times on the left side, and had performed the eighty–five gestures of greeting required by the social manual of the bush, and asked the three hundred and sixty–five questions de rigueur regarding the honorable health of his honorable horde of offspring, and his eye had fallen again on the red cards in his hand, the fact struck him that the relative was of precisely the same shade of complexion as himself. Could he set him down as he had many a mere red–blooded person and thereby perhaps establish a precedent that might result in his own mortification? Yet could he stretch a shade—or several shades—and set him down as "white"? No, there was the oath of office, and the government that administered it had been found long–armed and Argus–eyed. Long he sat in deepest meditation. Being a Panamanian, he could not of course know that Uncle Sam was in a hurry for his census. Till at length, as the sun was firing the western jungle tree–tops, a scintillating idea rewarded his unwonted cogitation. He caught up the medium soft pencil and wrote in aristocratic hand down across the sheet where other information is supposed to find place:

"Color;—A very light mixture," and taking his leave with the requisite seventy–five gestures and genuflexions, he drifted Empireward with the dozen cards the day had yielded.

Which is why I was shocked next morning by the disrespectful report of Renson that "my friend the boss had tied a can to the Spig's tail," and our dainty and lamented comrade went back to the more fitting blue–blood occupation of swinging a cane in the lobbies of Panama's famous hostelries.

But what mattered such small losses? Had not "Scotty" been engaged to fill the breach—or all of them, one or two breaches more or less made small difference to "Scotty." He was a cozy little barrel of a man, born in "Doombahrton," and for some years past had been dispensing good old Dumbarton English in Panama's proudest educational institution. But Panama's school vacation is during her "summer," her dry season from February to April. What more natural then than that "Scotty" should have concluded to pass his vacation taking census, for obviously—"a mon must pick up a wee bit o' change wherever he can."

I seemed to have been appointed to a purely sight–seeing job. One February noon I reported at the office to find that passes to Gatun had been issued to five of us, "Scotty," "Mac," Renson, and Barter among the number. The task in the "town by the dam site" it seemed, was proving too heavy for the regular enumerators of that district.

We left by the 2:10 train. Cascadas and Bas Obispo rolled away behind us, across the canal I caught a glimpse of the wilderness surrounding the abode of "Old Fritz," then we entered a to me unknown land. I could easily have fancied myself a tourist, especially so at Matachin when "Mac" solemnly attempted to "spring" on me the old tourist hoax of suicided Chinamen as the derivation of the town's name. Through Gorgona, the Pittsburg of the Zone with its acres of machine–shops, rumbled the train and plunged beyond into a deep, if not exactly rank, endless jungle. The stations grew small and unimportant. Bailamonos and San Pablo were withering and wasting away, "'Orca L'garto," or the Hanged Alligator was barely more than a memory, Tabernilla a mere heap of lumber being tumbled on flatcars bound for new service further Pacificward. Of Frijoles there remained barely enough to shudder at, with the collector's nasal bawl of "Free Holys!" and everywhere the irrepressible tropical greenery was already rushing back to engulf the pigmy works of man. It seemed criminally wasteful to have built these entire towns with all the detail and machinery of a well governed and fully furnished city from police station to salt cellars only to tear them down again and utterly wipe them out four or five years after their founding. A forerunner of what, in a few brief years, will have happened to all the Zone—nay, is not this the way of life itself?

For soon the Spillway at Gatun is to close its gates and all this vast region will be flooded and come to be Gatun Lake. Villages that were old when Pizarro began his swine–herding will be wiped out, even this splendid double–tracked railroad goes the way of the rest, for on February fifteenth, a bare few days away, it was to be abandoned and where we were now racing northwestward through brilliant sunshine and Atlantic breezes would soon be the bottom of a lake over which great ocean steamers will glide, while far below will be tall palm–trees and the spreading mangoes, the banana, king of weeds, gigantic ferns and—well, who shall say what will become of the brilliant parrots, the monkeys and the jaguars?

For nearly an hour we had not a glimpse of the canal, lost in the jungle to the right. Then suddenly we burst out upon the growing lake, now all but licking at the rails beneath us, the Zone city of Gatun climbing up a hillside on its edge and scattering over several more. To the left I caught my first sight of the world– famous locks and dam, and at 3:30 we descended at the stone station, first mile–post of permanency, for being out of reach of the coming flood it is built to stay and shows what Canal Zone stations will be in the years to come. There remained for me but seven miles of the Isthmus still unseen.

On the cement platform was a great foregathering of the census clans from all districts, whence we climbed to the broad porch of the administration building above. There before me, for the first time in—well, many months, spread the Atlantic, the Caribbean perhaps I should say, seeming very near, so near I almost fancied I could have thrown a stone to where it began and stretched away up to the bluish horizon, while the entrance to the canal where soon great ships will enter poked its way inland to the locks beside us. Across the tree–tops of the flat jungle, also seeming close at hand though the railroad takes seven miles—and thirty– five cents if you are no employee—to reach it, was Colon, the tops of whose low buildings were plainly visible above the vegetation. Not many "Zoners," I reflected, catch their first view of Colon from the veranda of the Administration Building at Gatun.

We had arrived with time to spare. Fully an hour we loafed and yarned and smoked before a whistle blew and long lines of little figures began to come up out of the depths and zigzag across the landscape until soon a line of laborers of every shade known to humanity began to form, pay–checks in hand; its double head at the pay–windows on the two sides of the veranda, its tail serpentining off down the hillside and away nearly to the edge of the mammoth locks. Packs of the yellow cards of Cristobal district in hand—a relief to eyes that had been staring for days at the pink ones of Empire—we lined up like birds of prey just beyond the windows. As the first laborer passed this, one—nay, several of us pounced upon him, for all plans we had laid to line up and take turns were thus quickly overthrown and wild competition soon reigned. From then on each dived in to snatch his prey and, dragging him to the nearest free space, began in some language or other: "Where d'ye live?"

That was the overwhelming problem,—in what language to address each victim. Barter, speaking only his nasal New Jersey, took to picking out negroes, and even then often turned away in disgust when he landed a Martinique or a Haytian. West Indian "English" alternated with a black patois that smelt at times faintly of French, muscular, bullet–headed negroes appeared slowly and laboriously counting their money in their hats, eagle–nosed Spaniards under the boina of the Pyrenees, Spaniards from Castile speaking like a gatling–gun in action, now and again even a snappy–eyed Andalusian with his s–less slurred speech, slow, laborious Gallegos, Italians and Portuguese in numbers, Colombians of nondescript color, a Slovak who spoke some German, a man from Palestine with a mixture of French and Arabic noises I could guess at, and scattered here and there among the others a Turk who jabbered the lingua franca of Mediterranean ports. I "got" all who fell into my hands. Once I dragged forth a Hindu, and shuddered with fear of a first failure. But he knew a bit of a strange English and I found I recalled six or seven words of my forgotten Hindustanee.

Then suddenly a flood of Greeks broke upon us, growing deeper with every moment. Above the pandemonium my companions were howling hoarsely and imploringly for the interpreter, while clutching their trembling victim by the slack of his labor–stained shirt lest he escape un–enrolled. The interpreter, in accordance with a well–known law of physics and the limitations of human nature, could not be in sixteen places at once. I crowded close, caught his words, memorized the few questions, and there was I with my "Poomaynes?" "Poseeton?" and "Padremaynos?" enrolling Greeks unassisted, not only that but haughtily acting as interpreter for my fellows—not only without having studied the tongue of Achilles but never even having graced a Greek letter fraternity.

Quick tropical twilight descended, and still the labor–smeared line wound away out of sight into the darkness, still workmen of every shade and tongue jingled their brass–checks timidly on the edge of the pay–window, from behind which came roaring noises that the Americans within fancied Spaniards, or Greeks, or Roumanians must understand because they were not English noises; still we pounced upon the paid as upon a tackling–dummy in the early days of spring practice.

The colossal wonder of it all was how these deep−chested, muscle− knotted fellows endured us, how they refrained from taking us up between a thumb and forefinger and dropping us over the veranda railing. For our attack lacked somewhat in gentle courtesy, notably so that of "the Rowdy." He was a chestless youth of the type that has grown so painfully prevalent in our land since the soft−hearted abolishment of the beech−rod of revered memory; of that all too familiar type whose proofs of manhood are cigarettes and impudence and discordant noise, and whose national superiority is demonstrated by the maltreating of all other races. But the enrolled were all, black, white, or mixed, far more gentlemen than we. Some, of brief Zone experience, were sheepish with fear and the wonder as to what new mandate this incomprehensible U. S. was perpetrating to match its strange sanitary laws that forbade a man even to be uncleanly in his habits, after the good old sacred right of his ancestors to remotest ages. Then, too, there was a Zone policeman in dressy, new−starched khaki treading with dangling club and the icy−eye of public appearance, waiting all too eagerly for some one to "start something." But the great percentage of the maltreated multitude were "Old Timers," men of four or five years of digging who had learned to know this strange creature, the American, and the world, too; who smiled indulgently down upon our yelping and yanking like a St. Bernard above the snapping puppy he well knows cannot seriously bite him.

Dense black night had fallen. Here and there lanterns were hung, under one of which we dragged each captive. The last passenger back to Empire roared away into the jungle night; still we scribbled on, "backed" a yellow card and dived again into the muscular whirlpool to emerge dragging forth by the collar a Greek, a Pole, or a West Indian. It was like business competition, in which I had an unfair advantage, being able to understand any jargon in evidence. When at last the pay−windows came down with a bang and an American curse, and the serpentining tail squirmed for a time in distress and died away, as a snake's tail dies after sundown, I turned in more than a hundred cards. To−morrow the tail would revive to form the nucleus of a new serpent, and we should return by the afternoon train to the lock city, and so on for several days to come.

It was after nine of a black pay−day night. We were hungry. "The Rowdy," familiar with the lay of the land, volunteered to lead the foraging expedition. We stumbled down the hill and away along the railroad. A faint rumbling that grew to a confused roar fell on our ears. We climbed a bank into a wild conglomeration of wood and tin architecture, nationalities, colors, and noises, and across a dark, bottomless gully from the high street we had reached lights flashed amid a very ocean of uproar. "The Rowdy," as if to make the campaign as real as possible, led us racing down into the black abyss, whence we charged up the further slope and came sweating and breathless into the rampant rough and tumble of pay– day night in New Gatun, the time and place that is the vortex of trouble on the Isthmus. Merely a short street of one of the half– dozen Zone towns in which liquor licenses are granted, lined with a few saloons and pool–rooms; but such a singing, howling, swarming multitude as is rivaled almost nowhere else, except it be on Broadway at the passing of the old year. But this mob, moreover, was fully seventy percent black, and rather largely French—and when black and French and strong drink mix, trouble sprouts like jungle seeds. Now and then Policeman G——drifted by through the uproar, holding his "sap" loosely as for ready use and often half consciously hitching the heavy No. 38 "Colt" under his khaki jacket a bit nearer the grasp of his right hand. I little knew how familiar every corner of this scene would one day be to me.

A Chinese grocer sold us bread and cheese. Down on the further corner of the hubbub we entered a Spanish saloon and spread ourselves over the "white" bar, adding beer to our humble collation. Beyond the lattice–work that is the "color line" in Zone dispensaries, West Indians were dancing wild, crowded "hoe– downs" and "shuffles" amid much howling and more liquidation; on our side a few Spanish laborers quietly sipped their liquor. The Marines of course were "busted." The rest of us scraped up a few odd "Spigoty" dimes. The Spanish bar–tender—who is never the "tough" his American counterpart strives to show himself—but merely a cheery good–fellow—drifted into our conversation, and when we found I had slept in his native village he would have it that we accept a round of Valdepenas. Which must have been potent, for it moved "Scotty" to unbutton an inner pocket and set up an entire bottle of amontillado. So midnight was no great space off when we turned out again into the howling night and, having helped Renson to reach a sleeping–place, scattered to the bachelor quarters that had been found for us and lay down for the few hours that remained before the 5:51 should carry us back to Empire.

At last I had crossed all the Isthmus and heard the wash of the Caribbean at my feet. It was the Sunday following our Gatun days, and nearly a month since my landing on the Zone. The morning train from Empire left me at the lake–side city for a run over locks and dam which the working days had not allowed, and there being no other train for hours I set off along the railroad to walk the seven miles to Colon. On either side lay hot, rampant jungle, low and almost swampy. It was noon when I reached the broad railroad yards and Zone storehouses of Mt. Hope and turned aside to Cristobal hotel.

Cristobal is built on the very fringe of the ocean with the roll of waves at the very edge of its windows, and a far−reaching view of the Caribbean where the ceaseless Zone breeze is born. There stands the famous statue of Columbus protecting the Indian maid, crude humor in bronze; for Columbus brought Indian maids anything but protection. Near at hand in the joyous tropical sunshine lay a great steamer that in another week would be back in New York tying up in sleet and ice. A western bronco and a lariat might perhaps have dragged me on board, with a struggle.

There is no more line of demarkation between Cristobal and Colon than between Ancon and Panama. A khaki−clad Zone policeman patrols one sidewalk, a black one in the sweltering dark blue uniform and heavy wintry helmet of the Republic of Panama lounges on the other side of a certain street; on one side are the "enumerated" tags of the census, on the other none. Cross the street and you feel at once a foreigner. It is distinctly unlawful to sell liquor on Sunday or to gamble at any time on the Canal Zone; it is therefore with something approaching a shock that one finds everything "wide open" and raging just across the street.

I wandered out past "Highball's" merry−go−round, where huge negro bucks were laughing and playing and riding away their month's pay on the wooden horses like the children they are, and so on to the edge of the sea. Unlike Panama, Colon is flat and square−blocked, as it is considerably darker in complexion with its large mixture of negroes from the Caribbean shores and islands. Uncle Sam seems to have taken the city's fine beach away from her. But then, she probably never took any other advantage of it than to turn it into a garbage heap as bad as once was Bottle Alley. On one end is a cement swimming pool with the announcement, "Only for gold employees of the I. C. C. or P. R. R. and guests of Washington Hotel." It is merely a softer way of saying, "Only white Americans with money can bathe here."

Then beyond are the great hospitals, second only to those of Ancon, the "white" wards built out over the sea, and behind them the "black" where the negroes must be content with second−hand breezes. Some of the costs of the canal are here,—sturdy black men in a sort of bed−tick pajamas sitting on the verandas or in wheel chairs, some with one leg gone, some with both. One could not but wonder how it feels to be hopelessly ruined in body early in life for helping to dig a ditch for a foreign power that, however well it may treat you materially, cares not a whistle− blast more for you than for its old worn−out locomotives rusting away in the jungle.

Under the beautiful royal palms beyond, all bent inland in the constant breeze are park benches where one can sit with the Atlantic spreading away to infinity before, breaking with its ages—old, mysterious roll on the shore just as it did before the European's white sails first broke the gleaming skyline. Out to sea runs the growing breakwater from Toro Point, the great wireless tower, yet just across the bay on a little jutting, dense—grown tongue of land is the jungle hut of a jungle family as utterly untouched by civilization as was the verdant valley of Typee on the day Melville and Toby came stumbling down into it from the hills above.

But meanwhile I was not getting the long hours of unbroken sleep the heavy mental toil of enumeration requires. Free government bachelor quarters makes strange bed—fellows—or at least room— fellows. Quartermasters, like justice, are hopelessly blind or I might have been assigned quarters upon the financial knoll where habits and hours were a bit more in keeping with my own. But a bachelor is a bachelor on the Zone, and though he be clerk to his highness "the Colonel" himself he may find himself carelessly tossed into a "rough—neck" brotherhood.

House 47 was distinctly an abode of "rough—necks." A "rough—neck," it may be essential to explain to those who never ate at the same table with one, is a bull—necked, whole—hearted, hard—headed, cast—iron fellow who can ride the beam of a snorting, rock—tearing steam—shovel all day, wrestle the night through with various starred Hennessey and its rivals, and continue that round indefinitely without once failing to turn up to straddle his beam in the morning. He seems to have been created without the insertion of nerves, though he is never lacking in "nerve." He is a fine fellow in his way, but you sometimes wish his way branched off from yours for a few hours, when bed—time or a mood for quiet musing comes. He is a man you are glad to meet in a saloon—if you are in a mood to be there—or tearing away at the cliffs of Culebra; but there are other places where he does not seem exactly to fit into the landscape.

House 47, I say, was a house of "rough—necks." That fact became particularly evident soon after supper, when the seven phonographs were striking up their seven kinds of ragtime on seven sides of us; and it was the small hours before the poker games, carried on in much the same spirit as Comanche warfare, broke up through all the house. Then, too, many a "rough—neck" is far from silent even after he has fallen asleep; and about the time complete quiet seemed to be settling down it was four—thirty; and a jarring chorus of alarm—clocks wrought new upheaval.

41

Then there was each individual annoyance. Let me barely mention two or three. Of my room–mates, "Mitch" had sat at a locomotive throttle fourteen years in the States and Mexico, besides the four years he had been hauling dirt out of the "cut." Youthful ambition "Mitch" had left behind, for though he could still look forward to forty, railroad rules had so changed in the States during his absence that he would have had to learn his trade over again to be able to "run" there. Moreover four years on the Zone does not make a man look forward with pleasure to a States winter. So "Mitch," like many another "Zoner," was planning to buy with the savings of his $210 a month "when the job is done" a chunk of land on some sunny slope of a southern state and settle down for an easy descent through old age. There was nothing objectionable about "Mitch"—except perhaps his preference for late–hour poker. But he had a way of stopping with one leg out of his trousers when at last all the house had calmed down and cots were ceasing to creak, to make some such wholly irrelevant remark as; "By——, that—— dispatcher give me 609 to–day and she wouldn't pull a greased string out of a knot–hole"—and thereby always hung a tale that was sure to range over half the track mileage of the States and wander off somewhere into the sandy cactus wilderness of Chihuahua at least before "Mitch" succeeded in getting out of the other trouser leg.

The cot directly across from my own groaned—occasionally—under the coarse–grained bulk of Tom. Tom was a "rough–neck" par excellence, so much so that even in a houseful of them he was known as "Tom the Rough–neck," which to Tom was high tribute. Some preferred to call him "Tom the Noisy." He was built like a steam caisson, or an oil–barrel, though without fat, with a neck that reminded you of a Miura bull with his head down just before the estoque; and when he neglected to button his undershirt—a not infrequent oversight—he displayed the hairy chest of a mammoth gorilla.

Tom's philosophy of getting through life was exactly the same as his philosophy of getting through a rocky hillside with his steam– shovel. When it came to argument Tom was invariably right; not that he was over–supplied with logic, but because he possessed a voice and the bellows to work it that could rise to the roar of his own steam–shovel on those weeks when he chose to enter the shovel competition, and would have utterly overthrown, drowned out, and annihilated James Stewart Mill himself.

Tom always should have had money, for your "rough–neck" on the Zone has decidedly the advantage over the white–collared college graduate when the pay–car comes around. But of course being a genuine "rough–neck" Tom was always deep in debt, except on the three days after pay–day, when he was rolling in wealth.

Once I fancied the bulk of my troubles was over. Tom disappeared, leaving not a trace behind—except his working–clothes tumbled on and about his cot. Then it turned out that he was not dead, but in Ancon hospital taking the Keeley cure; and one summer evening he blew in again, his "cure" effected—with a bottle in his coat pocket and two inside his vest. So the next day there was Tom celebrating his recovery all over House 47 and when next morning he did finally go back to his shovel there were scattered about the room six empty quart bottles each labeled "whiskey." Luckily Tom ran a shovel instead of a passenger train and could claw away at his hillside as savagely as he chose without any danger whatever, beyond that of killing himself or an odd "nigger" or two.

We had other treasures on exhibition in 47. There was "Shorty," for instance. "Shorty" was a jolly, ugly open–handed, four–eyed little snipe of a roughneck machinist who had lost "in the line of duty" two fingers highly useful in his trade. In consequence he was now, after the generous fashion of the I.C.C., on full pay for a year without work, providing he did not leave the Zone. And while "Shorty," like the great majority of us, was a very tolerable member of society under the ordinary circumstances of having to earn his "three squares a day," paid leisure hung most ponderously upon him.

The amusements in Empire are few—and not especially amusing. There is really only one unfailing one. That is slid in glass receptacles across a yellow varnished counter down on Railroad Avenue opposite Empire Machine Shops. So it happened that "Shorty" was gradually winning the title of a thirty–third degree "booze– fighter," and passengers on any afternoon train who took the trouble to glance in at a wide–open door just Atlanticward of the station might have beheld him with his back to the track and one foot slightly raised and resting lightly and with the nonchalance of long practice on a gas–pipe that had missed its legitimate mission. In fact "Shorty" had come to that point where he would rather be caught in church than found dead without a bottle on him, and arriving home overflowing with joy about midnight slept away most of the day in 47 that he might spend as much of the night as the early closing laws of the Zone permitted at the amusement headquarters of Empire.

With these few hints of the life that raged beneath the roof of 47 it may perhaps be comprehensible, without going into detail, why I came to contemplate a change of quarters. I detest a kicker. I have small use for any but the man who will take his allotted share with the rest of the world without either whining or snarling. Yet when an official government census enumerator falls asleep on the edge of a tenement washtub with a question dead on his lips, or solemnly sets down a crow–black Jamaican as "white," it is Uncle Sam who is suffering and time for correction.

But it is one thing for a Canal Zone employee to resolve to move, and quite another to carry out that resolution. Nero was a meek, unassertive, submissive, tractable little chap, keenly sensible to the sufferings of his fellows, compared with a Zone quartermaster. So the first time I ventured to push open the screen door next to the post office I was grateful to escape unmaimed. But at last, when I had done a whole month's penance in 47, I resorted to strategy. On March first I entered the dreaded precinct shielded behind "the boss" with his contagious smile, and the musical quartermaster of Empire was overthrown and defeated, and I marched forth clutching in one hand a new "assignment to quarters."

That night I moved. The new, or more properly the older, room was in House 35, a one–story building of the old French type, many of which the Americans revamped upon taking possession of the Isthmian junk–heap, across and a bit down the graveled street. It was a single room, with no roommate to question, which I might decorate and otherwise embellish according to my own personal idiosyncrasies. At the back, with a door between, dwelt the superintendent of the Zone telephone system, with a convenient instrument on his table. In short, fortune seemed at last to be grinning broadly upon me.

But—the sequel. I hate to mention it. I won't. It's absurdly commonplace. Commonplace? Not a bit of it. He was a champion, an artist in his specialty. How can I have used that word in connection with his incomparable performance? Or attempt to give a hint of life on the Canal Zone without mentioning the most conspicuous factor in it?

He lived in the next room south, a half–inch wooden partition reaching half–way to the ceiling between his pillow and mine. By day he lay on his back in the right hand seat of a locomotive cab with his hand on the throttle and the soles of his shoes on the boiler plate—he was just long enough to fit into that position without wrinkling. During the early evening he lay on his back in a stout Mission rocking–chair on the front porch of House 35, Empire, C.Z. And about 8 P. M. daily he retired within to lie on his back on a regulation I.C.C. metal cot—they are stoutly built —one pine half–inch from my own. Obviously twenty–four hours a day of such onerous occupation had left some slight effects on his figure. His shape was strikingly similar to that of a push–ball. Had he fallen down at the top of Ancon or Balboa hill it would have been an even bet whether he would have rolled down sidewise or endwise—if his general type of build and specifications will permit any such distinction.

When I first came upon him, reposing serenely in the porch rocking–chair on the cushion that upholstered his spinal column, I was pleased. Clearly he was no "rough–neck"—he couldn't have been and kept his figure. There was no question but that he was perfectly harmless; his stories ought to prove cheerful and laugh– provoking and kindly. His very presence seemed to promise to raise several degrees the merriment in that corner of House 85.

It did. Toward eight, as I have hinted, he transferred from rocking–chair to cot. He was not afflicted with troublesome nerves. At times he was an entire minute in falling asleep. Usually, however, his time was something under the half; and he slept with the innocent, undisturbed sleep of a babe for at least twelve unbroken hours, unless the necessity of getting across the "cut" to his engine absolutely prohibited. Just there was the trouble. His first gentle, slumberous breath sounded like a small boy sliding down the sheet–iron roof of 35. His second resembled a force of carpenters tearing out the half–grown partitions. His third—but mere words are an absurdity. At times the noises from his gorilla–like throat softened down till one merely fancied himself in the hog–corral of a Chicago stockyards; at others we prayed that we might at once be transferred there. A thousand times during the night we were certain he was on the very point of choking to death, and sat up in bed praying he wouldn't, and offering our month's salary to charity if he would; and through all our fatiguing anguish he snorted undisturbedly on. In House 35 he was known as "the Sloth." It was a gentle and kindly title.

There were a few inexperienced inmates who had not yet utterly given up hope. The long hours of the night were spent in solemn conference. Pounding on the walls with hammers, chairs, and shoe– heels was like singing a lullaby. One genius invented a species of foghorn which proved very effective—in waking up all Empire east of the tracks, except "the Sloth." Some took to dropping their heavier and more dispensable possessions over the partition. One memorable night a fellow–sufferer cast over a young dry–goods box which, bouncing from the snorer's figure to the floor, caused him to lose a beat—one; and the feat is still one of the proud memories of 35. On Sundays when all the rest of the world was up and shaved and breakfasted and off on the 8:39 of a brilliant, sunny day to Panama, "the Sloth" would be still imperturbably snorting and choking in the depths of his cot. And in the evening, as the train roamed back through the fresh cool jungle dusk and deposited us at Empire station, and we crossed the wooden bridge before the hotel and began to climb the graveled path behind, hoping against hope that we might find crape on that door, from the night ahead would break on our cars a sound as of a hippopotamus struggling wildly against going down for the third and last time.

Most annoying of all, "the Sloth" was not even a bona fide bachelor. He proudly announced that, though he was a model of marital virtue, he had not lived with his wife in many years. I never heard a man who knew him by night ask why. It was close upon criminal negligence on the part of the I.C.C. to overlook its opportunity in this matter. There were so many, many uninhabited hilltops on the Zone where a private Sloth-dwelling might have been slapped together from the remains of falling towns at Gatun end; near it a grandstand might even have been erected and admission charged. Or at least the daily climb to it would have helped to reduce a push-ball figure, and thereby have improved the general appearance of the Canal Zone force.

CHAPTER IV

One morning early in March "the boss" and I crossed the suspension bridge over the canal. A handcar and six husky negroes awaited us, and we were soon bumping away over temporary spurs through the jungle, to strike at length the "relocation" opposite the giant tree near Bas Obispo that marked the northern limit of our district.

The P.R.R., you will recall, has been operating across the Isthmus since 1855. When the United States took over the Zone in 1904 it built a new double-tracked line of five-foot gauge for nearly the whole forty-seven miles. Much of this, however, runs through territory soon to be covered by Gatun Lake, nearly all the rest of it is on the wrong side of the canal. An almost entirely new line, therefore, is being built through the virgin jungle on the South American side of the canal, which is to be the permanent line and is known in Zone parlance as the "relocation." This is forty-nine miles in length from Panama to Colon, and is single track only, as freight traffic especially is expected, very naturally, to be lighter after the canal is opened. Already that portion from the Chagres to the Atlantic had been put in use—on February fifteenth, to be exact; and the time was not far off when the section within our district—from Gamboa to Pedro Miguel—would also be in operation.

That portion runs through the wilderness a mile or more back from the canal, through jungled hills so dense with vegetation one could only make one's way through it with the ubiquitous machete of the native jungle–dweller, except where tiny trails appear that lead to squatters' thatched huts thrown together of tin, dynamite and dry–goods boxes and jungle reeds in little scattered patches of clearing. Some of these hills have been cut half away for the new line—great generous "cuts," for to the giant 90–ton steam– shovels a few hundred cubic yards of earth more or less is of slight importance. All else is virtually impenetrable jungle. Travelers by rail across the Isthmus, as no doubt many ships' passengers will be in the years to come while their steamer is being slowly raised and lowered to and from the eighty–five–foot lake, will see little of the canal,—a glimpse of the Bas Obispo "cut" at Gamboa and little else from the time they leave Gatun till they return to the present line at Pedro Miguel station. But in compensation they will see some wondrous jungle scenery,—a tangled tropical wilderness with great masses of bush flowers of brilliant hues, gigantic ferns, countless palm and banana trees, wonderfully slender arrow–straight trees rising smooth and branchless more than a hundred feet to end in an immense bouquet of brilliant purplish–hue blossoms.

"The boss" barely noticed these things. One quickly grows accustomed to them. Why, Americans who have been down on the Zone for a year don't know there's a palm–tree on the Isthmus—or at least they do not remember there were no palm–trees in Keokuk, Iowa, when they left there.

Along this new–graveled line, still unused except by work–trains, we rode in our six negro–power car, dropping off in the gravel each time we caught sight of any species of human being. Every little way was a gang, averaging some thirty men, distinct in nationality,—Antiguans shoveling gravel, Martiniques snarling and quarreling as they wallowed thigh–deep in swamps and pools, a company of Greeks unloading train–loads of ties, Spaniards leisurely but steadily grading and surfacing, track bands of "Spigoties" chopping away the aggressive jungle with their machetes—the one task at which the native Panamanian (or Colombian, as many still call themselves) is worth his brass– check. Every here and there we caught labor's odds and ends, diminutive "water–boys," likewise of varying nationality, a negro switch–boy dozing under the bit of shelter he had rigged up of jungle ferns, frightening many a black laborer speechless as we pounced upon him emerging from his "soldiering" in the jungle; occasionally even a native bushman on his way to market from his palm-thatched home generations old back in the bush, who has scarcely noticed yet that the canal is being dug, fell into our hands and was inexorably set down in spite of all protest unless he could prove beyond question that he had already been "taken" or lived beyond the Zone line.

Thus we scribbled incessantly on, even through the noon hour, dragging gangs one by one away from their tasks, shaking laborers out of the brief after-lunch siesta in a patch of shade. "The boss" was hampered by having only two languages where ten were needed. In the early afternoon he went on to Paraiso to feed himself and the traction power, while I held the fort. Soon after rain fell, a sort of advance agent of the rainy season, a sudden tropical downpour that ran in rivulets down across the pink cardboards and my victims. Yet strange to note, the writing of the medium soft pencil remained as clear and unsmudged as in the driest weather, and so clean a rain was it that it did not even soil my white cotton shirt. I continued unheeding, only to note with surprise a few minutes later that the sun was shining on the dense green jungle about me as brilliantly as ever and that I was dry again as when I had set out in the morning.

"The boss" returned, and when I had eaten the crackers and the bottle of pink lemonade he brought, we pushed on toward the Pacific. Till at length in mid-afternoon we came to the top of the descent to Pedro Miguel and knew that the end of our district was at hand. So powerful was the breeze from the Atlantic that our six man-power engine sweated profusely as they toiled against it, even on the downgrade of the return to Empire.

To "Scotty" had been assigned my Empire "recalls" and I had been given a new and virgin territory,—namely, the town of Paraiso. It lies "somewhat back from the village street," that is, the P.R.R. Indeed, trains do not deign to notice its existence except on Sundays. But there is the temporary bridge over the canal which few engineers venture to "snake her across" at any great speed, and the enumerator housed in Empire need not even be a graduate "hobo" to be able to drop off there a bit after seven in the morning and prance away up the chamois path into the town.

Wherever on the Zone you espy a town of two-story skeleton screened buildings scattered over hills, with winding gravel roads and trees and flowers between there you may be sure live American "gold" employees. Yet somehow the Canal Commission had dodged the monotony you expected, somehow they have broken up the grim lines that make so dismal the best-intentioned factory town. There are hints that the builders have

48

heard somewhere of the science of landscape gardening. At times these same houses are deceiving, for all I. C. C. buildings bear a strong family resemblance, and it is only at the door that you know whether it is bachelors' quarters, a family residence, or the supreme court.

From the outside world "P'reeso" scarcely draws a glance of attention; but once in it you find a whole Zone town with all the accustomed paraphernalia of I. C. C. hotel and commissary, hospital and police station, all ruled over and held in check by the famous "Colonel" in command of the latter. Moreover Paraiso will some day come again into her own, when the "relocation" opens and brings her back on the main line, while proud Culebra and haughty Empire, stranded on a railless shore of the canal, will wither and waste away and even their broad macadamed roads will sink beneath a second–growth jungle.

Renson had come to lend assistance. He set to work among the negro cabins, the upper gallery seats of Paraiso's amphitheater of hills, for Renson had been a free agent for more than a month now and was not exactly in a condition to interview American housewives. My own task began down at the row of inhabited box– cars, and so on through shacks and tenements with many Spanish laborers' wives. Then toward noon the labor–train screamed in, with two "gold" coaches and many open cattle–cars with long benches jammed with sweaty workmen, easily six hundred men in the six cars, who swept in upon the town like a flood through a suddenly opened sluiceway as the train barely paused and shrieked away again.

Renson and I dashed for the laborers' mess–halls, where hundreds of sun–bronzed foreigners, divided only as to color, packed pell– mell around a score of wooden tables heavily stocked with rough and tumble food—yet so different from the old French catch as catch can days when each man owned his black pot and toiled all through the noon–hour to cook himself an unsanitary lunch. We jotted them down at express speed, with changes of tongue so abrupt that our heads were soon reeling, and in the place where our minds should have been sounded only a confused chaotic uproar like a wrangling within the covers of a polyglot dictionary. Then suddenly I landed a Russian! It was the final straw. I like to speak Spanish, I can endure the creaking of Turks attempting to talk Italian, I can bend an ear to the excruciating "French" of Martinique negroes, I have boldly faced sputtering Arabs, but I will NOT run the risk of talking Russian. It was the second and last case during my census days when I was forced to call for interpretative assistance.

At best we caught only a small percentage at each table before the crowd had wolfed and melted away. An odd half dozen more, perhaps, we found stretched out in the shade under the mess–hall and neighboring quarters before the imperative screech of the labor–train whistle ended a scene that must be several times repeated, and now left us silent and alone, to wander wet and weary to the nearest white bachelor quarters, there to lie on our backs an hour or more till the polyglot jumble of words in the back of our heads had each climbed again to its proper shelf.

Speaking of white bachelor quarters, therein lay the enumerator's greatest problem. The Spaniard or the Jamaican is in nine cases out of ten fluently familiar with his companion's antecedents and pedigree. He can generally furnish all the information the census department calls for. But it is quite otherwise with the American bachelor. He may know his room–mate's exact degree of skill at poker, he probably knows his private opinion of "the Colonel," he is sure to know his degree of enmity to the prohibition movement; but he is not at all certain to know his name and rarely indeed has he the shadow of a notion when and in what particular corner of the States he began the game of existence. So loose are ties down on the Zone that a man's room–mate might go off into the jungle and die and the former not dream of inquiring for him for a week. Especially we world–wanderers, as are a large percentage of "Zoners," with virtually no fixed roots in any soil, floating wherever the job suggests or the spirit moves, have the facts of our past in our own heads only. No wanderer of experience would dream of asking his fellow where he came from. The answer would be too apt to be, "from the last place." So difficult did this matter become that I gave up rushing for the bus to Pedro Miguel each evening and the even more distressing necessity of catching that premature 6:30 train each morning in Empire and, packing a sheet and pillow and tooth–brush, moved down to Paraiso that I might spend the first half of the night in quest of these elusive bits of bachelor information.

Meanwhile the enrolling by day continued unabated. I had my first experience enumerating "gold" married quarters—white American families; just enough for experience and not enough to suffer severely. The enrolling of West Indians was pleasanter. The wives of locomotive engineers and steam–shovel cranemen were not infrequently supercilious ladies who resented being disturbed during their "social functions" and lacked the training in politeness of Jamaican "mammies." Living in

Paradise now under a paternal all–providing government, they seemed to have forgotten the rolling–pin days of the past. It was here in Paraiso that I first encountered that strange, that wondrous strange custom of lying about one's age. Negro women never did. What more absurd, uncalled–for piece of dishonesty! Does Mrs. Smith fear that Mrs. Jones next door will succeed in pumping out of me that capital bit of information? Little does she know the long prison sentence at "hard labor" that stares me in the face for any such slip; to say nothing of my naturally incommunicative disposition. Or is she ashamed to let ME know the truth?—unaware that all such information goes in at my ears and down my pencil to the pink card before me like a message over the wires, leaving no more trace behind. Surely she must know that I care not a pencil–point whether she is eighteen or fifty–two, nor remember which one minute after her screen door has slammed behind me—unless she has caused me to glance up in wonder at her silvering temples of thirty–five when she simpers "twenty–two"—and to set her down as forty to be on the safe side. Oh now, please, ladies, do not understand me as accusing the American wives of Paraiso in general of this weakness. The large majority were quite pleasant, frank, and overflowing with cheery good sense. But the percentage who were not was far larger than I, who am also an American, was pleased to find it.

But doubly astonishing were the few cases of lying by proxy. A "clean–cut," college–graduated civil engineer of thirty–two whom one would have cited as an example of the best type of American, gave all data concerning himself in an unimpeachable manner. His wife was absent. When the question of her age arose he gave it, with the slightest catch in his voice, as twenty. Now that might be all very well. Men of thirty–two are occasionally so fortunate as to marry girls of twenty. But a moment later the gentleman in question finds himself announcing that his wife has been living on the Zone with him since 1907; and that she was born in New England! Thus is he tripped over his own clothes–line. For New England girls do not marry at fifteen; mother would not let them even if they would.

I, too, had gradually worked my way high up among the nondescript cabins on the upper rim of Paraiso that seem on the very verge of pitching headlong into the noisy, smoky canal far below with the jar of the next explosion, when one sunny mid–afternoon I caught sight of Renson dejectedly trudging down across what might be called the "Maiden" of Paraiso, back of the two-story lodge–hall. I took leave of my ebony hostess and descended. Renson's troubles were indeed disheartening. Back in the jungle fringe of the town he had fallen into a swarm of Martiniques, and Renson's French being nothing more than an unstudied mixture of English and Spanish, he had not gathered much information. Moreover negro women from the French isles are enough to frighten any virtuous young Marine.

"What's the sense o' me tryin' to chew the fat in French?" asked Renson, with tears in his voice. "I ain't in no condition to work at this census business any longer anyway. I ain't got to bed before three in the morning this week"—in his air was open suggestion that it was some one else's fault—"Some day I'll be gettin' in bad, too. This mornin' a fool nigger woman asked me if I didn't want her black pickaninny I was enumeratin', thinkin' it was a good joke. You know how these bush kids is runnin' around all over the country before a white man's brat could walk on its hind legs. 'Yes,' I says, 'if I was goin' alligator huntin' an' needed bait!' I come near catchin' the brat up by the feet an' beatin' its can off. I'm out o' luck any way, an'—"

The fact is Renson was aching to be "fired." More than thirty days had he been subject only to his own will, and it was high time he returned to the nursery discipline of camp. Moreover he was out of cigarettes. I slipped him one and smoothed him down as its fumes grew—for Renson was as tractable as a child, rightly treated—and set him to taking Jamaican tenements in the center of town, while I struck off into the jungled Martinique hills myself.

There were signs abroad that the census job was drawing to a close. My first pay–day had already come and gone and I had strolled up the gravel walk one noon–day to the Disembursing Office with my yellow pay certificate duly initialed by the examiner of accounts, and was handed my first four twenty–dollar gold pieces—for hotel and commissary books sadly reduce a good paycheck. Already one evening I had entered the census office to find "the boss" just peeling off his sweat–dripping undershirt and dotted with skin–pricking jungle life after a day mule–back on the thither side of the canal; an utterly fruitless day, for not only had he failed during eight hours of plunging through the wilderness to find a single hut not already decorated with the "enumerated" tag, but not even a banana could he lay hands on when the noon–hour overhauled him far from the ministrations of "Ben" and the breeze–swept veranda of Empire hotel.

It was, I believe, the afternoon following Renson's linguistic troubles that "the boss" came jogging into Paraiso on his sturdy mule. In his eagerness to "clean up" the territory we fell to corraling negroes everywhere, in the streets, at work, buying their supplies at the commissary, sleeping in the shade of wayside trees, anywhere and everywhere, until at last in his excitement "the boss" let his medium soft pencil slip by the column for color and dashed down the abbreviation for "mixed" after the question, "Married or Single?" Which may have been near enough the truth of the case, but suggested it was time to quit. So we marked Paraiso "finished except for recalls" and returned to Empire.

One by one our fellow-enumerators had dropped by the wayside, some by mutual agreement, some without any agreement whatever. Renson was now relieved from census duty, to his great joy, there remained but four of us,—"the boss" and "Mac" in the office, "Scotty" and I outside. A deep conference ensued and, as if I had not had good luck enough already, it was decided that we two should go through the "cut" itself. It was like offering us a salary to view all the Great Work in detail, for virtually all the excavation of any importance on the Zone lay within the confines of our district.

So one day "Scotty" and I descended at the girderless railroad bridge and, taking each one side of the canal, set out to canvass its every nook and cranny. The canal as it then stood was about the width of two city blocks, an immense chasm piled and tumbled with broken rock and earth, in the center a ditch already filled with grimy water, on either side several levels of rough rock ledges with sheer rugged stone faces; for the hills were being cut away in layers each far above the other. High above us rose the jagged walls of the "cut" with towns hanging by their fingernails all along its edge, and ahead in the abysmal, smoky distance the great channel gashed through Culebra mountain.

The different levels varied from ten to twenty feet one above the other, each with a railroad on it, back and forth along which incessantly rumbled and screeched dirt-trains full or empty, halting before the steam-shovels, that shivered and spouted thick black smoke as they ate away the rocky hills and cast them in great giant handsful on the train of one-sided flat-cars that moved forward bit by bit at the flourish of the conductor's yellow flag. Steam-shovels that seemed human in all except their mammoth fearless strength tore up the solid rock with snorts of rage and the panting of industry, now and then flinging some troublesome, stubborn boulder angrily upon the cars. Yet they could be dainty as human fingers too, could pick up a railroad spike or push a rock gently an inch further across the car. Each was run by two white Americans, or at least what would prove such when they reached the shower-bath in their quarters—the craneman far out on the shovel arm, the engineer within the machine itself with a labyrinth of levers demanding his unbroken attention. Then there was of course a gang of negroes, firemen and the like, attached to each shovel.

All the day through I climbed and scrambled back and forth between the different levels, dodging from one track to another and along the rocky floor of the canal, needing eyes and ears both in front and behind, not merely for trains but for a hundred hidden and unknown dangers to keep the nerves taut. Now and then a palatial motorcar, like some rail–road breed of taxi, sped by with its musical insistent jingling bells, usually with one of the countless parties of government guests or tourists in spotless white which the dry season brings. Dirt–trains kept the right of way, however, for the Work always comes first at Panama. Or it might be the famous "yellow car" itself with members of the Commission. Once it came all but empty and there dropped off inconspicuously a man in baggy duck trousers, a black alpaca coat of many wrinkles; and an unassuming straw hat, a white–haired man with blue—almost babyish blue–eyes, a cigarette dangling from his lips as he strolled about with restless yet quiet energy. There has been no flash and glitter of military uniforms on the Zone since the French sailed for home, but every one knew "the Colonel" for all that, the soldier who has never "seen service," who has never heard the shrapnel scream by overhead, yet to whom the world owes more thanks than six conquering generals rolled into one.

Scores of "trypod" and "Star" drills, whole battalions of deafening machines run by compressed air brought from miles away, are pounding and grinding and jamming holes in the living rock. After them will presently come nonchalantly strolling along gangs of the ubiquitous black "powder–men" and carelessly throw down boxes of dynamite and pound the drill–holes full thereof and tamp them down ready to "blow" at 11:30 and 5:30 when the workmen are out of range,—those mighty explosions that twelve times a week set the porch chairs of every I.C.C. house on the Isthmus to rocking, and are heard far out at sea.

Anywhere near the drills is such a roaring and jangling that I must bellow at the top of my voice to be heard at all. The entire gamut of sound–waves surrounds and enfolds me, and with it all the powerful Atlantic breeze sweeps deafeningly through the channel. Down in the bottom of the canal if one step behind anything that shuts off the breeze it is tropically hot; yet up on the edge of the chasm above, the trees are always nodding and bowing before the ceaseless wind from off the Caribbean. Scores of "switcheros" drowse under their sheet–iron wigwams, erected not so much as protection from the sun, for the drowsers are mostly negroes and immune to that, as from young rocks that the dynamite blasts frequently toss a quarter−mile. Then over it all hang heavy clouds of soft−coal dust from trains and shovels, shifting down upon the black, white and mixed, and the enumerator alike; a dirty, noisy, perilous, enjoyable job.

Everywhere are gangs of men, sometimes two or three gangs working together at the same task. Shovel gangs, track gangs, surfacing gangs, dynamite gangs, gangs doing everything imaginable with shovel and pick and crowbar, gangs down on the floor of the canal, gangs far up the steep walls of cut rock, gangs stretching away in either direction till those far off look like upright bands of the leaf−cutting ants of Panamanian jungles; gangs nearly all, whatever their nationality, in the blue shirts and khaki trousers of the Zone commissary, giving a peculiar color scheme to all the scene.

Now and then the boss is a stony−eyed American with a black cigar clamped between his teeth. More often he is of the same nationality as the workers, quite likely from the same town, who jabbers a little imitation English. Which is one of the reasons why a force of "time inspectors" is constantly dodging in and out over the job, time−book and pencil in hand, lest some fellow− townsman of the boss be earning his $1.50 a day under the shade of a tree back in the jungle. Here are Basques in their boinas, preferring their native "Euscarra" to Spanish; French "niggers" and English "niggers" whom it is to the interest of peace and order to keep as far apart as possible; occasionally a few sunburned blond men in a shovel gang, but they prove to be Teutons or Scandinavians; laborers of every color and degree—except American laborers, more than conspicuous by their absence. For the American negro is an untractable creature in large numbers, and the caste system that forbids white Americans from engaging in common labor side by side with negroes is to be expected in an enterprise of which the leaders are not only military men but largely southerners, however many may be shivering in the streets of Chicago or roaming hungrily through the byways of St. Louis. It is well so, perhaps. None of us who feels an affection for the Zone would wish to see its atmosphere lowered from what it is to the brutal depths of our railroad construction camps in the States.

The attention of certain state legislatures might advantageously be called to the Zone Spaniard's drinking−cup. It is really a tin can on the end of a long stick, cover and all. The top is punched sieve−like that the water may enter as it is dipped in the bucket with which the water−boy strains along. In the bottom is a single small hole out of which spurts into the drinker's mouth a little stream of water as he holds it high above his head, as once he drank wine from his leather bota in far−off Spain. Many a Spanish gang comes entirely from the same town, notably Salamanca or Avila. I set them to staring and chattering by some simple remark about their birthplace: "Fine view from the Paseo del Rastro, eh?" "Does the puente romano still cross the river?" But I had soon to cease such personalities, for picks and shovels lay idle as long as I remained in sight and Uncle Sam was the loser.

So many were the gangs that I advanced barely a half–mile during this first day and, lost in my work, forgot the hour until it was suddenly recalled by the insistent, strident tooting of whistles that forewarns the setting–off of the dynamite charges from the little red electric boxes along the edge of the "cut." I turned back toward Paraiso and, all but stumbling over little red–wound wires everywhere on the ground, dodging in and out, running forward, halting or suddenly retreating, I worked my way gradually forward, while all the world about me was upheaving and spouting and belching forth to the heavens, as if I had been caught in the crater of a volcano as it suddenly erupted without warning. The history of Panama is strewn with "dynamite stories." Even the French had theirs in their sixteen per cent, of the excavation of Culebra; in American annals there is one for every week. Three days before, one of my Empire friends set off one afternoon for a stroll through the "cut" he had not seen for a year. In a retired spot he came upon two negroes pounding an irregular bundle. "What you doing, boys?" he inquired with idle curiosity. "Jes' a brealdn' up dis yere dynamite, boss," languidly answered one of the blacks. My friend was one of those apprehensive, over–cautious fellows so rare on the Zone. Without so much as taking his leave he set off at a run. Some two car–lengths beyond an explosion pitched him forward and all but lifted him off his feet. When he looked back the negroes had left. Indeed neither of them has reported for work since.

Then there was "Mac's" case. In his ambition for census efficiency "Mac" was in the habit of stopping workmen wherever he met them. One day he encountered a Jamaican carrying a box of dynamite on his head and, according to his custom, shouted:

"Hey, boy! Had your census taken yet?"

"What dat, boss?" cried the Jamaican with wide–open eyes, as he threw the box at "Mac's" feet and stood at respectful attention.

Somehow "Mac" lacked a bit of his old zealousness thereafter.

On the second day I pushed past Cucaracha, scene of the greatest "slide" in the history of the canal when forty–seven acres went into the "cut," burying under untold tons of earth and rock steam– shovels and railroads, "Star" and "trypod" drills, and all else in sight—except the "rough–necks," who are far too fast on their feet to be buried against their will. One by one I dragged shovel gangs away to a distance where my shouting could be heard, one by one I commanded drillmen to shut off their deafening machines, all day I dodged switching, snorting trains, clambered by steep rocky paths, or ladders from one level to another, howling above the roar of the "cut" the time–worn questions, straining my ear to catch the answer. Many a negro did not know the meaning of the word "census," and must have it explained to him in words of one syllable. Many a time I climbed to some lofty rock ledge lined with drills and, gesticulating like a semaphore in signal practice, caught at last the wandering attention of a negro, to shout sore–throated above the incessant pounding of machines and the roaring of the Atlantic breeze:

"Hello, boy! Census taken yet?"

A long vacant stare, then at last, perhaps, the answer:

"Oh, yes sah, boss."

"When and where?"

"In Spanish Town, Jamaica, three year ago, sah."

Which was not an attempt to be facetious but an answer in all seriousness. Why should not one census, like one baptism, suffice for a life–time? It was fortunate that enumerators were not accustomed to carry deadly weapons.

Quick changes from negro to Spanish gangs demonstrated beyond all future question how much more native intelligence has the white man. Rarely did I need to ask a Spaniard a question twice, still less ask him to repeat the answer. His replies came back sharp and swift as a pelota from a cesta. West Indians not only must hear the question an average of three times but could seldom give the simplest information clearly enough to be intelligible, though ostensibly speaking English. A Spanish card one might fill out and be gone in less time than the negro could be roused from his racial torpor. Yet of the Spaniards on the Zone surely seventy per cent, were wholly illiterate, while the negroes from the British Weat Indies, thanks to their good fortune in being ruled over by the world's best colonist, could almost invariably read and write; many of those shoveling in the "cut" have been trained in trigonometry.

Few are the "Zoners" now who do not consider the Spaniard the best workman ever imported in all the sixty—five years from the railroad surveying to the completion of the canal. The stocky, muscle—bound little fellows come no longer to America as conquistadores, but to shovel dirt. And yet more cheery, willing workers, more law—abiding subjects are scarcely to be found. It is unfortunate we could not have imported Spaniards for all the canal work; even they have naturally learned some "soldiering" from the example of lazy negroes who, where laborers must be had, are a bit better than no labor—though not much.

The third day came, and high above me towered the rock cliffs of Culebra's palm—crowned hill, steam—shovels approaching the summit in echelon, here and there an incipient earth and rock "slide" dribbling warningly down. He who still fancies the digging of the canal an ordinary task should have tramped with us through just our section, halting to speak to every man in it, climbing out of this man—made canon twice a day, a strenuous climb even near its ends, while at Culebra one looks up at all but unscalable mountain walls on either side.

From time to time we hear murmurs from abroad that Americans are making light of catastrophies on the Isthmus, that they cover up their great disasters by a strict censorship of news. The latter is mere absurdity. As to catastrophies, a great "slide" or a premature dynamite explosion are serious disaster to Americans on the job just as they would be to Europeans. But whereas the continental European would sit down before the misfortune and weep, the American swears a round oath, spits on his hands, and pitches in to shovel the "slide" out again. He isn't belittling the disasters; it is merely that he knows the canal has got to be dug and goes ahead and digs it. That is the greatest thing on the Zone. Amid all the childish snarling of "Spigoties," the back— biting of Europe, the congressional wrangles, the Cabinet politics, the man on the job,—"the Colonel," the average American, the "rough—neck"—goes right on digging the canal day by day as if he had never heard a rumor of all this outside noise.

Mighty is the job from one point of view; yet tiny from another. With all his enormous equipment, his peerless ingenuity, and his feverish activity all little man has succeeded in doing is to scratch a little surface wound in Mother Earth, cutting open a few superficial veins, of water, that trickle down the rocky face of the "cut."

By March twelfth we had carried our task past and under Empire suspension bridge, and the end of the "cut" was almost in sight. That day I clawed and scrambled a score of times up the face of rock walls. I zigzagged through long rows of negroes pounding holes in rock ledges. I stumbled and splashed my way through gangs of Martinique "muckers." I slid down the face of government-made cliffs on the seat of my commissary breeches. I fought my way up again to stalk through long lines of men picking away at the dizzy edge of sheer precipices. I rolled down in the sand and rubble of what threatened to develop into "slides." I crawled under snorting steam-shovels to drag out besooted negroes—negroes so besooted I had to ask them their color—while dodging the gigantic swinging shovel itself, to say nothing of "dhobie" blasts and rocks of the size of drummers' trunks that spilled from it as it swung. I climbed up into the quivering monster itself to interrupt the engineer at his levers, to shout at the craneman on his beam. I sprang aboard every train that was not running at full speed, walking along the running-board into the cab; if not to "get" the engineer at least to gain new life from his private ice-water tank. I scrambled over tenders and quarter-miles of "Lidgerwood flats" piled high with broken rock and earth, to scream at the American conductor and his black brakemen, often to find myself, by the time I had set down one of them, carried entirely out of my district, to Pedro Miguel or beyond the Chagres, and have to "hit the grit" in "hobo" fashion and catch something back to the spot where I left off. In short I poked into every corner of the "cut" known to man, bawling in the November-first voice of a presidential candidate to everything in trousers:

"Eh! 'Ad yer census taken yet?"

And what was my reward? From the northern edge of Empire to where the "cut" sinks away into the Chagres and the low, flat country beyond, I enrolled—just thirteen persons. It was then and there, though it still lacked an hour of noon, that I ceased to be a census enumerator. With slow and deliberate step I climbed out of the canal and across a pathed field to Bas Obispo and, sitting down in the shade of her station, patiently awaited the train that would carry me back to Empire.

Four thousand, six hundred and seventy-seven Zone residents had I enrolled during those six weeks. Something over half of these were Jamaicans. Of the states Pennsylvania was best represented. Martinique negroes, Greeks, Spaniards, and Panamanians were some eighty per cent illiterate; of some three hundred of the first only a half dozen even claimed to read and write; and non–wedlock was virtually universal among them.

Rumor has it that there are seventy–two separate states and dependencies represented on the Isthmus. My own cards showed a few less. Most conspicuous absences, besides American negroes, were natives of Honduras, of four countries of South America, of most of Africa, and of entire Australia. That this was largely due to chance was shown by the fact that my fellow–enumerators found persons from all these countries.

I had enrolled persons born in the following places: All the United States except three or four states in the far northwest; Canada, Mexico, Guatemala, Salvador, Nicaragua, Costa Rica, Panama, Canal Zone, Colombia, Venezuela, British Guiana (Demarara), French and Dutch Guiana, Ecuador, Peru, Bolivia and Chile, Cuba, Hayti and Santo Domingo, Jamaica, Barbados, St. Vincent, Trinidad, Saint Lucia, Montserrat, Dominica, Nevis, Nassau, Eleuthera and Inagua, Martinique, Guadalupe, Saint Thomas (Danish West Indies), Curacao and Tobago, England, Ireland, Scotland, Holland, Finland, Belgium, Denmark, Sweden, Norway, Russia, France, Spain, Andorra, Portugal, Switzerland, Germany, Italy, Austria, Hungary, Greece, Servia, Turkey, Canary Islands, Syria, Palestine, Arabia, India (from Tuticorin to Lahore), China, Japan, Egypt, Sierra Leone, South Africa and—the High Seas.

"Where you born, boy?" I had run across a wrinkled old negro who had worked more than thirty years for the P.R.R.

"'Deed ah don' know, boss,"

"Oh, come! Don't know where you were born?" "Fo' Gawd, boss, ah's tellin' yo de truff. Ah don know, 'cause ah born to sea."

"Well, what country are you a subject of?"

"Truly ah cahn't say, boss."

"Well what nationality was your father?"

"Ah neveh see him, sah." "Well then where the devil did you first land after you were born?"

"'Deed ah cahn't say, boss. T'ink it were one o' dem islands. Reckon ah's a subjec' o' de' worl', boss."

Weeks afterward the population of Uncle Sam's ten by fifty–mile strip of tropics was found to have been on February first, 1912, 62,810. No, anxious reader, I am not giving away inside information; the source of my remarks is the public prints. Of these about 25,000 were British subjects (West Indian negroes with very few exceptions). Of the entire population 37,428 were employed by the U. S. government. Of white Americans, of the Brahmin caste of the "gold" roll, there were employed on the Zone but 5,228,

CHAPTER V

Police headquarters presented an unusual air of preoccupation next morning. In the corner office the telephone rang often and imperatively, several times erect figures in khaki and broad "Texas" hats flashed by the doorway, the drone of earnest conference sounded a few minutes, and the figures flashed as suddenly out again into the world. In the inner office I glanced once more in review through the "Rules and Regulations." The Zone, too, was now familiar ground, and as for the third requirement for a policeman—to know the Zone residents by sight—a strange face brought me a start of surprise, unless it beamed above the garb that shouted "tourist." Now all I needed was a few hours of conference and explanation on the duties, rights, and privileges of policemen; and that of course would come as soon as leisure again settled down over headquarters.

Musing which I was suddenly startled to my feet by "the Captain" appearing in the doorway.

"Catch the next train to Balboa;" he said. "You've got four minutes. You'll find Lieutenant Long on board. Here are the people to look out for."

He thrust into my hands a slip of paper, from another direction there was tossed at me a new brass–check and "First–Class Private" police badge No. 88, and I was racing down through Ancon. In the meadow below the Tivoli I risked time to glance at the slip of paper. On it were the names of an ex–president and two ministers of a frowsy little South American republic during whose rule a former president and his henchmen had been brutally murdered by a popular uprising in the very capital itself.

In the first–class coach I found Lieutenant Long, towering so far above all his surroundings as to have been easily recognized even had he not been in uniform. Beside him sat Corporal Castillo of the "plain–clothes" squad, a young man of forty, with a high forehead, a stubby black mustache, and a chin that was decisive without being aggressive.

"Now here's the Captain's idea," explained the Lieutenant, as the train swung away around Ancon hill, "We'll have to take turns mounting guard over them, of course. I'll have to talk Spanish, and nobody'd have to look at Castillo more than once to know he was born up in some crack in the Andes."—Which was one of the Lieutenant's jokes, for the Corporal, though a Colombian, was as white, sharp–witted, and energetic as any American on the Zone. —"But no one to look at him would suspect that Fr—French, is it?"

"Franck."

"Oh, yes, that Franck could speak Spanish. We 'll do our best to inflate that impression, and when it comes your turn at guard– mount you can probably let several little things of interest drift in at your ears."

"I left headquarters before the Captain had time to explain," I suggested.

"Oh!" said the Lieutenant. "Well, here it is in a spectacle–case, as our friend Kipling would put it. We're on our way to Culebra Island. There are now in quarantine there three men who arrived yesterday from South America. They are members of the party of the murdered president. To–day there will arrive and also be put in hock the three gents whose names you have there. Now we have a private inside hunch that the three already here have come up particularly and specifically to prepare for the funeral of the three who are arriving. Which is no hair off our brows, except it's up to us to see they don't pull off any little stunts of that kind on Zone territory."

At least this police business was starting well; if this was a sample it would be a real job.

Zone Policeman 88

The train had stopped and we were climbing the steps of Balboa police station; for without the co-operation of the "Admiral of the Pacific Fleet" we could not reach Culebra Island.

"By the way, I suppose you're well armed?" asked the Lieutenant in his high querulous voice, as we drank a last round of ice-water preparatory to setting out again.

"Em—I've got a fountain pen," I replied. "I haven't been a policeman twenty minutes yet, and I was appointed in a hurry."

"Fine!" cried "the Admiral" sarcastically, snatching open the door of a closet beside the desk. "With a warm job like this on hand! You know what these South Americans are—" with a wink at the Lieutenant that was meant also for Castillo, who stood with his felt hat on the back of his head and a far-away look in his eyes.

"Yah, mighty dangerous—around meal time," said the Corporal; though at the same time he drew from a hip pocket a worn leather holster containing a revolver, and examined it intently.

Meanwhile "the Admiral" had handed me a massive No. 88 "Colt" with holster, a box of cartridges, and a belt that might easily have served as a horse's saddle-girth. When I had buckled it on under my coat the armament felt like a small boy clinging about my waist.

We trooped on down a sort of railroad junction with a score of abandoned wooden houses. It was here I had first landed on the Zone one blazing Sunday nearly two months before and tramped away for some miles on a rusty sandy track along a canal already filled with water till a short jungle path led me into my first Zone town. Already that seemed ancient history.

The police launch, manned by negro prisoners, with "the Admiral" in a cushioned arm-chair at the wheel, was soon scudding away across the sunlit harbor, the breakwater building of the spoil of Culebra "cut" on our left, ahead the cluster of small islands being torn to pieces for Uncle Sam's fortifications. The steamer being not yet sighted, we put in at Naos Island, where the bulky policeman in charge led us to dinner at the I. C. C. hotel, during which the noonday blasting on the Zone came dully across to us. Soon after we were landing at the cement sidewalk of the island— where I had been a prisoner for a day

63

in January as my welcome to U. S. territory—and were being greeted by the pocket edition doctor and the bay–windowed German who had been my wardens on that occasion.

We found the conspirators at a table in a corridor of the first– class quarantine station. In the words of Lieutenant Long "they fully looked the part," being of distinctly merciless cut of jib. They were roughly dressed and without collars, convincing proof of some nefarious design, for when the Latin–American entitled to wear them leaves off his white collar and his cane he must be desperate indeed.

We "braced" them at once, marching down upon them as they were murmuring with heads together over a mass of typewritten sheets. The Corporal was delegated to inform them in his most urbane and hidalguezco Castilian that we were well acquainted with their errand and that we were come to frustrate by any legitimate means in our power the consummation of any such project on American territory. When the first paralyzed stare of astonishment that plans they had fancied locked in their own breasts were known to others had somewhat subsided, one of them assumed the spokesmanship. In just as courtly and superabundant language he replied that they were only too well aware of the inadvisability of carrying out any act against its sovereignty on U. S. soil; that so long as they were on American territory they would conduct themselves in a most circumspect and caballeroso manner—"but," he concluded, "in the most public street of Panama city the first time we meet those three dogs—we shall spit in their faces— that's all, nada mas," and the blazing eyes announced all too plainly what he meant by that figure of speech.

That was all very well, was our smiling and urbane reply, but to be on the safe side and merely as a matter of custom we were under the unfortunate necessity of requesting them to submit to the annoyance of having their baggage and persons examined with a view to discovering what weapons—

"Como no senores? All the examination you desire." Which was exceedingly kind of them. Whereupon, when the Lieutenant had interpreted to me their permission, we fell upon them and amid countless expressions of mutual esteem gave them and their baggage such a "frisking" as befalls a Kaffir leaving a South African diamond mine, and found them armed with—a receipt from the quarantine doctor for "one pearl–handled Smill and Wilson No. 32." Either they really intended to postpone their little affair until they reached Panama, or they had succeeded in concealing their weapons elsewhere.

The doctor and his assistant were already being rowed out to the steamer that was to bring the victims. They were to be lodged in a room across the corridor from the conspirators, which corridor it would be our simple duty to patrol with a view to intercepting any exchange of stray lead. We fell to planning such division of the twenty-four hours as should give me the most talkative period. The Lieutenant took the trouble further to convince the trio of my total ignorance of Spanish by a distinct and elaborate explanation, in English, of the difference between the words "muchacho" and "muchacha." Then we wandered down past the grimy steerage station to the shore end of the little wharf to await the doctor and our proteges.

The ocean breeze swept unhampered across the island; on its rocky shore sounded the dull rumble of waves, for the sea was rolling a bit now. The swelling tide covered inch by inch a sandy ridge that connected us with another island, gradually drowning beneath its waters several rusty old hulls. A little rocky wooded isle to the left cut off the future entrance to the canal. Some miles away across the bay on the lower slope of a long hill drowsed the city of Panama in brilliant sunshine; and beyond, the hazy mountainous country stretched southwestward to be lost in the molten horizon. On a distant hill some Indian was burning off a patch of jungle to plant his corn.

Meanwhile the Lieutenant and the Corporal had settled some Lombroso proposition and fallen to reciting poetry. The former, who was evidently a lover of melancholy, mouth-filling verse, was declaiming "The Raven" to the open sea. I listened in wonder. Was this then police talk? I had expected rough, untaught fellows whose conversation at best would be pornographic rather than poetic. My astonishment swelled to the bursting point when the Colombian not only caught up the poem where the Lieutenant left off but topped it off with that peerless translation by Bonalde the Venezuelan, beginning:

Una fosca media noche, cuando en tristes reflexiones
Sobre mas de un raro infolio de olvidados cronicones—

And just then the quarantine launch swung around the neighboring island. I tightened my horse belt and dragged the "Colt" around within easy reach; and a moment later the doctor and his bulking understudy stepped ashore—alone.

"They didn't come," said the former; "they were not allowed to leave their own country."

"Hell and damnation," said the Lieutenant at length in a calm, conversational tone of voice, with the air of a small boy who has been wantonly robbed of a long–promised holiday but who is determined not to make a scene over it. The Corporal seemed indifferent, and stood with the far–away look in his eyes as if he were already busy with some other plans or worries. But then, the Corporal was married. As for myself, I had somehow felt from the first that it was too good to be true. Adventure has steadily dodged me all my days.

A half–hour later we were pitching across the bay toward Ancon hill, scaled bare on one end by the work of fortification like a Hindu hair–cut. The water came spitting inboard now and then, and dejected silence reigned within the craft. But spirits gradually revived and before we could make out the details of the wharf the Corporal's hearty genuine laughter and the Lieutenant's rousing carcajada were again drifting across the water. At Balboa I unburdened myself of my shooting hardware and, catching the labor– train, was soon mounting the graveled walk to Ancon police station. In the second–story squad–room of the bungalow were eight beds. But there were more than enough policemen to go round, and the legal occupant of the bunk I fell asleep in returned from duty at midnight and I transferred to the still warm nest of a man on the "grave–yard" shift.

"It's customary to put a man in uniform for a while first before assigning him to plain–clothes duty," the Inspector was saying next morning when I finished the oath of office that had been omitted in the haste of my appointment, "but we have waived that in your case because of the knowledge of the Zone the census must have given you."

Thus casually was I robbed of the opportunity to display my manly form in uniform to tourists of trains and the Tivoli—tourists, I say, because the "Zoners" would never have noticed it. But we must all accept the decrees of fate.

That was the full extent of the Inspector's remarks; no mention whatever of the sundry little points the recruit is anxious to be enlightened upon. In government jobs one learns those details by experience. For the time being there was nothing for me to do but to descend to the "gum–shoe" desk in Ancon station and sit in the swivel–chair opposite Lieutenant Long "waiting for orders."

Toward noon a thought struck me. I swung the telephone around and "got" the Inspector.

"All my junk is up in Empire yet," I remarked.

"All right, tell the desk—man down there to make you out a pass. Or—hold the wire! As long as you're going out, there's a prisoner over in Panama that belongs up in Empire. Go over and tell the Chief you want Tal Fulano."

I wormed my way through the fawning, neck—craning, many—shaded mob of political henchmen and obsequious petitioners into the sacred hushed precincts of Panama police headquarters. A paunched "Spigoty" with a shifty eye behind large bowed glasses, vainly striving to exude dignity and wisdom, received me with the oily smirk of the Panamanian office—holder who feels the painful necessity of keeping on outwardly good terms with all Americans. I flashed my badge and mentioned a name. A few moments later there was presented to me a sturdy, if somewhat flabby, young Spaniard carefully dressed and perfumed. We bowed like life—long acquaintances and, stepping down to the street, entered a cab. The prisoner, which he was now only in name, was a muscular fellow with whom I should have fared badly in personal combat. I was wholly unarmed, and in a foreign land. All those sundry little unexplained points of a policeman's duty were bubbling up within me. When the prisoner turned to remark it was a warm day should I warn him that anything he said would be used against him? When he ordered the driver to halt before the "Panazone" that he might speak to some friends should I fiercely countermand the order? What was my duty when the friends handed him some money and a package of cigars? Suppose he should start to follow his friends inside to have a drink—but he didn't. We drove languidly on down the avenue and up into Ancon, where I heaved a genuine sigh of relief as we crossed the unmarked street that made my badge good again. The prisoner was soon behind padlocks and the money and cigars in the station safe. These and him and the transfer card I took again with me into the foreign Republic in time for the evening train. But he seemed even more anxious than I to attract no attention, and once in Empire requested that we take the shortest and most inconspicuous route to the police station; and my responsibility was soon over.

Many were the Z.P. facts I picked up during the next few days in the swivel—chair. The Zone Police force of 1912 consisted of a Chief of Police, an Assistant Chief, two Inspectors, four Lieutenants, eight sergeants, twenty corporals, one hundred and seventeen "first—class policemen," and one hundred and sixteen "policemen" (West

Indian negroes without exception, though none but an American citizen could aspire to any white position); not to mention five clerks at headquarters, who are quite worth the mentioning. "Policemen" wore the same uniform as "first–class" officers, with khaki–covered helmet instead of "Texas" hat and canvas instead of leather leggings, drew one–half the pay of a white private, were not eligible for advancement, and with some few notable exceptions were noted for what they did know and the facility with which they could not learn. One Inspector was in charge of detective work and the other an overseer of the uniformed force. Each of the Lieutenants was in charge of one– fourth of the Zone with headquarters respectively at Ancon, Empire, Gorgona, and Cristobal, and the sub–stations within these districts in charge of sergeants, corporals, or experienced privates, according to importance.

Years ago when things were yet in primeval chaos and the memorable sixth of February of 1904 was still well above the western horizon there was gathered together for the protection of the newly–born Canal Strip a band of "bad men" from our ferocious Southwest, warranted to feed on criminals each breakfast time, and in command of a man–eating rough–rider. But somehow the bad men seemed unable to transplant to this new and richer soil the banefulness that had thrived so successfully in the land of sage–brush and cactus. The gourmandizing promised to be chiefly at the criminal tables; and before long it was noted that the noxious gentlemen were gradually drifting back to their native sand dunes, and the rough–riding gave way to a more orderly style of horsemanship. Then bit by bit some men—just men without any qualifying adjective whatever— began to get mixed up in the matter; one after another army lieutenants were detailed to help the thing along, until by and by they got the right army lieutenant and the right men and the Z. P. grew to what it is to–day,—not the love, perhaps, but the pride of every "Zoner" whose name cannot be found on some old "blotter."

There are a number of ways of getting on the force. There is the broad and general high–way of being appointed in Washington and shipped down like a nice fresh vegetable in the original package and delivered just as it left the garden without the pollution of alien hands. Then there's the big, impressive, broad–shouldered fellow with some life and military service behind him, and the papers to prove it, who turns up on the Zone and can't help getting on if he takes the trouble to climb to headquarters. Or there are the special cases, like Marley for instance. Marley blew in one summer day from some uncharted point of the compass with nothing but his hat and a winning smile on his brassy features, and naturally soon drifted up the "Thousand Stairs." But Marley wasn't exactly of that manly build that takes "the Chief" and "the Captain" by storm; and there were suggestions on his young–old face that he had seen perhaps a trifle too much of life. So he wiped the sweat from his brow several times at the third–story landing only to find as often that the expected vacancy was not yet. Meanwhile the tropical days slipped idly by and Marley's "standin" with the owners of I. C. C. hotel–books began to strain and threaten to break away, and everything sort of gave up the ghost and died. Everything, that is, except the winning smile. 'Til one afternoon with only that asset left Marley met the department head on the grass–bordered path in front of the Episcopal chapel, just where the long descent ends and a man begins to regain his tractable mood, and said Marley:

"Say, looka here, Chief. It's a question of eats with me. We can't put this thing off much longer or—"

Which is why that evening's train carried Marley, with a police badge and the little flat volume bound in imitation leather in his pocket, out to some substation commander along the line for the corporal in charge to break in and hammer down into that finished product, a Zone Policeman.

Incidentally Marley also illustrated some months later one of the special ways of getting off the force. It was still simpler. Going "on pass" to Colon to spend a little evening, Marley neglected to leave his No. 38 behind in the squad–room, according to Z. P. rules. Which was careless of him. For when his spirits reached that stage where he recognized what sport it would be to see the "Spigoty" policemen of Bottle Alley dance a western cancan he bethought him of the No. 38. Which accounts for the fact that the name of Marley can no longer be found on the rolls of the Z. P. But all this is sadly anticipating.

Obviously, you will say, a force recruited from such dissimilar sources must be a thing of wide and sundry experience. And obviously you are right. Could a man catch up the Z. P. by the slack of the khaki riding breeches and shake out their stories as a giant in need of carfare might shake out their loose change, then might he retire to some sunny hillside of his own and build him a sound–proof house with a swimming pool and a revolving bookcase and a stable of riding horses, and cause to be erected on the front lawn a kneeling–place where publishers might come and bow down and beat their foreheads on the pavement.

There are men in the Z. P. who in former years have played horse with the startled markets of great American cities; men whose voices will boom forth in the pulpit and whisper sage councils in the professional in years to come; men whom doting parents have sent to Harvard—on whom it failed to take, except on their clothes—men who have gone down into the Valley of the Shadow of Death and crawled on hands and knees through the brackish red brook that runs at the bottom and come out again smiling on the brink above. Careers more varied than Mexican sombreros one might hear in any Z. P. squad–room—were not the Z. P. so much more given to action than to autobiography.

They bore little resemblance to what I had expected. My mental picture of an American policeman was that conglomerate average one unconsciously imbibes from a distant view of our city forces, and by comparison with foreign,—a heavy–footed, discourteous, half–fanatical, half–irreligious clubber whose wits are as slow as his judgment is honest. Instead of which I found the Z. P. composed almost without exception of good–hearted, well set up young Americans almost all of military training. I had anticipated, from other experiences, a constant bickering and a general striving to make life unendurable for a new–comer. Instead I was constantly surprised at the good fellowship that existed throughout the force. There were of course some healthy rivalries; there were no angels among them—or I should have fled the Isthmus much earlier; but for the most part the Z. P. resembled nothing so much as a big happy family. Above all I had expected early to make the acquaintance of "graft," that shifty–eyed monster which we who have lived in large American cities think of as sitting down to dinner with the force in every mess–hall. Graft? Why a Zone Policeman could not ride on a P. R. R. train in full uniform when off duty without paying his fare, though he was expected to make arrests if necessary and stop behind with his prisoner. Compared indeed with almost any other spot on the broad earth's surface "graft" eats slim meals on the Canal Zone.

The average Zone Policeman would arrest his own brother—which is after all about the supreme test of good policehood. He is not a man who likes to keep "blotters," make out accident reports and such things, that can be of interest only to those with clerks' and bookkeepers' souls.

He would far rather be battling with sun, man, and vegetation in the jungle. He is of those who genuinely and frankly have no desire to become rich, and "successful," a lack of ambition that formal society cannot understand and fancies a weakness.

Zone Policeman 88

I had still another police surprise during these swivel–chair days. I discovered there was on the Zone a yellow tailor who made Beau Brummel uniforms at $7.50, compared with which the $5 ready– made ones were mere clothes. All my life long I had been laboring under the delusion that a uniform is merely a uniform. But one lives and learns.

There are few left, I suppose, who have not heard that gray– bearded story of the American in the Philippines who called his native servant and commanded:

"Juan, va fetch the caballo from the prado and—and—oh, saddle and bridle him. Damn such a language anyway! I'm sorry I ever learned it."

This is capped on the Zone by another that is not only true but strikingly typical. An American boss who had been much annoyed by unforeseen absences of his workmen pounced upon one of his Spaniards one morning crying:

"When you know por la noche that you're not going to trabaja por la manana why in—don't you habla?"

"Si, senor," replied the Spaniard.

By which it may be gathered that linguistic ability on the Zone is on a par with that in other U. S. possessions. Of the seven of us assigned to plain–clothes duty on this strip of seventy–two nationalities there was a Colombian, a gentleman of Swedish birth, a Chinaman from Martinique, and a Greek, all of whom spoke English, Spanish, and at least one other language. Of the three native Americans two spoke only their mother tongue. In the entire white uniformed force I met only Lieutenant Long and the Corporal in charge of Miraflores who could seriously be said to speak Spanish, though I am informed there were one or two others.

This was not for a moment any fault of the Z. P. It comes back to our government and beyond that to the American people. With all our expanding over the surface of the earth in the past fourteen years there still hangs over us that old provincial back–woods bogie, "English is good enough for me." We have only to recall what England does for those of her colonial servants who want seriously to study the language of some portion of her subjects to have something very like the blush of shame creep up the back of our necks. Child's task as is the learning of a foreign language, provincial old Uncle Sam just flat—foots along in the same old way, expecting to govern and judge and lead along the path of civilization his foreign colonies by bellowing at them in his own nasal drawl and treating their tongue as if it were some purely animal sound. He is well personified by Corporal——, late of the Z. P. The Corporal had served three years in the Philippines and five on the Zone, and could not ask for bread in the Spanish tongue. "Why don't you learn it?" some one asked one day.

"Awe," drawled the Corporal, "what's the use o' goin' t' all that trouble? If you have t' have any interpretin' done all you got t' do is t' call in a nigger."

Uncle Sam not merely lends his servants no assistance to learn the tongues of his colonies, but should one of his subjects appear bearing that extraordinary accomplishment he gives him no preference whatever, no better position, not a copper cent more salary; and if things get to a pass where a linguist must be hired he gives the job to the first citizen that comes along who can make a noise that is evidently not English, or more likely still to some foreigner who talks English like a mouthful of Hungarian goulash. It is not the least of the reasons why foreign nations do not take us as seriously as they ought, why our colonials do not love us and, what is of far greater importance, do not advance under our rule as they should.

Meanwhile there had gradually been reaching me "through the proper channels," as everything does on the Zone even to our ice—water, the various coupon—books and the like indispensable to Zone life and the proper pursuit of plain—clothes duty. Distressing as are statistics the full comprehension of what might follow requires the enumeration of the odds and ends I was soon carrying about with me.

A brass—check; police badge; I. C. C. hotel coupon—book; Commissary coupon—book; "120—Trip Ticket" (a booklet containing blank passes between any stations on the P. R. R., to be filled out by holder) Mileage book (purchased by employees at half rates of 2 1/2 cents a mile for use when traveling on personal business) "24—Trip Ticket" (a free courtesy pass to all "gold" employees allowing one monthly round trip excursion over any portion of the line) Freight—train pass for the P. R. R.; Dirt—train and locomotive pass for the Pacific division; ditto for the Central division; likewise for the Atlantic division; (in short about everything on wheels was free to the "gum—shoe" except the "yellow car") Passes admitting to docks and steamers at either end of the Zone; note—book; pencil or pen; report cards and envelopes (one of which the plain—clothes man must fill out and forward to headquarters "via train–guard" wherever night may overtake him— "the gum–shoe's day's work," as the idle uniformed man facetiously dubs it).

Furthermore the man out of uniform is popularly supposed never to venture forth among the populace without:

Belt, holster, cartridges, and the No. 38 "Colt" that reminds you of a drowning man trying to drag you down; handcuffs; police whistle; blackjack (officially he never carries this; theoretically there is not one on the Isthmus. But the "gum–shoe" naturally cannot twirl a police club, and it is not always policy to shoot every refractory prisoner). Then if he chances to be addicted to the weed there is the cigarette–case and matches; a watch is frequently convenient; and incidentally a few articles of clothing are more or less indispensable even in the dry season. Now and again, too, a bit of money does not come amiss. For though the Canal Zone is a Utopia where man lives by work–coupons alone, the detective can never know at what moment his all–embracing duties may carry him away into the foreign land of Panama; and even were that possibility not always staring him in the face, in the words of "Gorgona Red," "You've got t' have money fer yer booze, ain't ye?"

Which seems also to be Uncle Sam's view of the matter. Far and away more important than any of the plain–clothes equipment thus far mentioned is the "expense account." It is unlike the others in that it is not visible and tangible but a mere condition, a pleasant sensation like the consciousness of a good appetite or a youthful fullness of life. The only reality is a form signed by the czar of the Zone himself tucked away among I. C. C. financial archives. That authorizes the man assigned to special duty in plain clothes to be reimbursed money expended in the pursuance of duty up to the sum of $60 per month; though it is said that the interpretation of this privilege to the full limit is not unlikely to cause flames of light, thunderous rumblings, and other natural phenomena in the vicinity of Empire and Culebra. But please note further; these expenditures may be only "for cab or boat hire, meals away from home, and LIQUOR and CIGARS!" Plainly the "gum–shoe" should be a bachelor.

Fortunately, however, the proprietor of the expense account is not required personally to consume it each month. It is designed rather to win the esteem of bar–tenders, loosen the tongues of suspects, libate the thirsty stool–pigeon, and prime other accepted sources of information. But beware! Exceeding care in filling out the account of such expenditures at the month's end. Carelessness leads a hunted life on the Canal Zone. Take, for instance, the slight error of my friend—who, having made such expenditure in Colon, by a slip of the pen, or to be nice, of the typewriter, sent in among three score and ten items the following:

Feb. 4/ 2 bots beer; Cristobal........50c

and in the course of time found said voucher again on his desk with a marginal note of mild–eyed wonder and more than idle curiosity, in the handwriting of a man very high up indeed;

WHERE can you buy beer in Cristobal?

All this and more I learned in the swivel–chair waiting for orders, reading the latest novel that had found its way to Ancon station, and receiving frequent assurances that I should be quite busy enough once I got started. Opposite sat Lieutenant Long pouring choice bits of sub–station orders into the 'phone:

"Don't you believe it. That was no accident. He didn't lose everything he had in every pocket rolling around drunk in the street. He's been systematically frisked. Sabe frisked? Get on the job and look into it."

For the Lieutenant was one of those scarce and enviable beings who can live with his subordinates as man to man, yet never find an ounce of his authority missing when authority is needed.

Now and then a Z. P. story whiled away the time. There was the sad case of Corporal———–in charge of———–station. Early one Sunday afternoon the Corporal saw a Spaniard leading a goat along the railroad. Naturally the day was hot. The Corporal sent a policeman to arrest the inhuman wretch for cruelty to animals. When he had left the culprit weeping behind padlocks he went to inspect the goat, tied in the shade under the police station.

"Poor little beast," said the sympathetic Corporal, as he set before it a generous pan of ice–water fresh from the police station tank. The goat took one long, eager, grateful draught, turned over on its back, curled up like the sensitive–plants of Panama jungles when a finger touches them, and departed this vale of tears. But Corporal——–was an artist of the first rank. Not only did he "get away with it" under the very frowning battlements of the judge, but sent the Spaniard up for ten days on the charge against him. Z. P.'s who tell the story assert that the Spaniard did not so much mind the sentence as the fact that the Corporal got his goat.

Then there was "the Mystery of the Knocked–out Niggers." Day after day there came reports from a spot out along the line that some negro laborer strolling along in a perfectly reasonable manner suddenly lay down, threw a fit, and went into a comatose state from which he recovered only after a day or two in Ancon or Colon hospitals. The doctors gave it up in despair. As a last resort the case was turned over to a Z. P. sleuth. He chose him a hiding– place as near as possible to the locality of the strange manifestation. For half the morning he sweltered and swore without having seen or heard the slightest thing of interest to an old "Zoner." A dirt–train rumbled by now and then. He strove to amuse himself by watching the innocent games of two little Spanish switch–boys not far away. They were enjoying themselves, as guileless childhood will, between their duties of letting a train in and out of the switch. Well on in the second half of the morning another diminutive Iberian, a water–boy, brought his compatriots a pail of water and carried off the empty bucket. The boys hung over the edge of the pail a sort of wire hook, the handle of their home–made drinking–can, no doubt, and went on playing.

By and by a burly black Jamaican in shirt–sleeves loomed up in the distance. Now and then as he advanced he sang a snatch of West Indian ballad. As he espied the "switcheros" a smile broke out on his features and he hastened forward his eyes fixed on the water– pail. In a working species of Spanish he made some request of the boys, the while wiping his ebony brow with his sleeve. The boys protested. Evidently they had lived on the Zone so long they had developed a color line. The negro pleaded. The boys, sitting in the shade of their wigwam, still shook their heads. One of them was idly tapping the ground with a broom–handle that had lain beside him. The negro glanced up and down the track, snatched up the boys' drinking vessel, of which the wire hooked over the pail was not after all the handle, and stooped to dip up a can of water. The little fellow with the broom–stick, ceasing a useless protest, reached a bit forward and tapped dreamily the rail in front of him. The Jamaican suddenly sent the can of water some rods down the track, danced an artistic buck–and–wing shuffle on the thin air above his head, sat down on the back of his neck, and after trying a moment in vain to kick the railroad out by the roots, lay still.

By this time the sleuth was examining the broom–handle. From its split end protruded an inch of telegraph wire, which chanced also to be the same wire that hung over the edge of the galvanized bucket. Close in front of the innocent little fellows ran a "third rail!"

Then suddenly this life of anecdote and leisure ended. There was thrust into my hands a typewritten–sheet and I caught the next thing on wheels out to Corozal for my first investigation. It was one of the most commonplace cases on the Zone. Two residents of my first dwelling–place on the Isthmus had reported the loss of $150 in U. S. gold.

Easier burglary than this the world does not offer. Every bachelor quarters on the Isthmus, completely screened in, is entered by two or three screen–doors, none of which is or can be locked. In the building are from twelve to twenty–four wide–open rooms of two or three occupants each, no three of whom know one another's full names or anything else, except that they are white Americans and ipso facto (so runs Zone philosophy) above dishonesty. The quarters are virtually abandoned during the day. Two negro janitors dawdle about the building, but they, too, leave it for two hours at mid–day. Moreover each of the forty–eight or more occupants probably has several friends or acquaintances or enemies who may drift in looking for him at any hour of the day or night. No negro janitor would venture to question a white American's errand in a house; Panama is below the Mason and Dixon line. In practice any white American is welcome in any bachelor quarters and even to a bed, if there is one unoccupied, though he be a total stranger to all the community. Add to this that the negro tailor's runner often has permission to come while the owner is away for suits in need of pressing, that John Chinaman must come and claw the week's washing out from under the bed where the "rough–neck" kicked it on Saturday night, that there are a dozen other legitimate errands that bring persons of varying shades into the building, and above all that the bachelors themselves, after the open–hearted old American fashion, have the all but universal habit of tossing gold and silver, railroad watches and real–estate bonds, or anything else of whatever value, indifferently on the first clear corner that presents itself. Precaution is troublesome and un–American. It seems a fling at the character of your fellow bachelors—and in the vast majority of Zone cases it would be. But it is in no sense surprising that among the many thousands that swarm upon the Isthmus there should be some not averse to increasing their income by taking advantage of these guileless habits and bucolic conditions. There are suggestions that a few— not necessarily whites—make a profession of it. No wonder "our chief trouble is burglary" and has been ever since the Z. P. can remember. Summed up, the pay–day gold that has thus faded away is perhaps no small amount; compared with what it might have been under prevailing conditions it is little.

As for detecting such felonies, police officers the world around know that theft of coin of the realm in not too great quantities is virtually as safe a profession as the ministry. The Z. P. plain–clothes man, like his fellows elsewhere, must usually be content in such cases with impressing on the victim his Sherlockian astuteness, gathering the available facts of the case, and return to typewrite his report thereof to be carefully filed away among headquarters archives. Which is exactly what I had to do in the case in question, diving out the door, notebook in hand, to catch the evening train to Panama.

I was growing accustomed to Ancon and even to Ancon police–mess when I strolled into headquarters on Saturday, the sixteenth, and the Inspector flung a casual remark over his shoulder:

"Better get your stuff together. You're transferred to Gatun."

I was already stepping into a cab en route for the evening train when the Inspector chanced down the hill.

"New Gatun is pretty bad on Saturday nights," he remarked. (All too well I remembered it.) "The first time a nigger starts anything run him in, and take all the witnesses in sight along."

"That reminds me; I haven't been issued a gun or handcuffs yet," I hinted.

"Hell's fire, no?" queried the Inspector. "Tell the station commander at Gatun to fix you up."

CHAPTER VI

I scribbled myself a ticket and was soon rolling northward, greeting acquaintances at every station. The Zone is like Egypt; whoever moves must travel by the same route. At Pedro Miguel and Cascadas armies of locomotives—the "mules" of the man from Arkansas—stood steaming and panting in the twilight after their day's labor and the wild race homeward under hungry engineers. As far as Bas Obispo this busy, teeming Isthmus seemed a native land; beyond, was like entering into foreign exile. It is a common Zone experience that only the locality one lives in during his first weeks ever feels like "home."

The route, too, was a new one. From Gorgona the train returned crab–wise through Matachin and across the sand dyke that still holds the Chagres out of the "cut," and halted at Gamboa cabin. Day was dying as we rumbled on across the iron bridge above the river and away into the fresh jungle night along the rock– ballasted "relocation." The stillness of this less inhabited half of the Zone settled down inside the car and out, the evening air of summer caressing almost roughly through the open windows. The train continued its steady way almost uninterruptedly, for though new villages were springing up to take the place of the old sinking into desuetude and the flood along with the abandoned line, there were but two where once were eight. We paused at the new Frijoles and the box–car town of Monte Lirio and, skirting on a higher level with a wide detour on the flanks of thick jungled and forested hills what is some day to be Gatun Lake, drew up at 7:30 at Gatun.

I wandered and inquired for some time in a black night—for the moon was on the graveyard shift that week—before I found Gatun police station on the nose of a breezy knoll. But for "Davie," the desk–man, who it turned out was also to be my room–mate, and a few wistful–eyed negroes in the steel–barred room in the center of the building, the station was deserted. "Circus," said the desk–man briefly. When I mentioned the matter of weapons he merely repeated the word with the further information that only the station commander could issue them.

There was nothing to do therefore but to ramble out armed with a lead pencil into a virtually unknown town riotous with liquor and negroes and the combination of Saturday night, circus time, and the aftermath of pay–day, and to strut back and forth in a way to suggest that I was a perambulating arsenal. But though I wandered a long two hours into every hole and corner where trouble might have its breeding–place, nothing but noise took place in my sight and hearing. I turned disgustedly away toward the tents pitched in a grassy valley between the two Gatuns. At least there was a faint hope that the equestrienne might assault the ring–master.

I approached the tent flap with a slightly quickening pulse. World–wide and centuries old as is the experience, personally I was about to "spring my badge" for the first time.

78

Suppose the doortender should refuse to honor it and force me to impress upon him the importance of the Z. P.—without a gun? Outwardly nonchalant I strolled in between the two ropes. Proprietor Shipp looked up from counting his winnings and opened his mouth to shout "ticket!" I flung back my coat, and with a nod and a half-wink of wisdom he fell back again to computing his lawful gains.

By the way, are not you who read curious to know, even as I for long years wondered, where a detective wears his badge? Know then that long and profound investigation among the Z. P. seems to prove conclusively that as a general and all but invariable rule he wears it pinned to the lining of his coat, or under his lapel, or on the band of his trousers, or on the breast of his shirt, or in his hip pocket, or up his sleeve, or at home on the piano, or riding around at the end of a string in the baby's nursery; though as in the case of all rules this one too has its exceptions.

Entertainments come rarely to Gatun. The one-ringed circus was packed with every grade of society from gaping Spanish laborers to haughty wives of dirt-train conductors, among whom it was not hard to distinguish in a far corner the uniformed sergeant in command of Gatun and the long lean corporal tied in a bow-line knot at the alleged wit of the versatile but solitary clown who changed his tongue every other moment from English to Spanish. But the end was already near; excitement was rising to the finale of the performance, a wrestling match between a circus man and "Andy" of Pedro Miguel locks. By the time I had found a leaning-place it was on—and the circus man of course was conquered, amid the gleeful howling of "rough-necks," who collected considerable sums of money and went off shouting into the black night, in quest of a place where it might be spent quickly. It would be strange indeed if among all the thousands of men in the prime of life who are digging the canal at least one could not be found who could subjugate any champion a wandering circus could carry among its properties. I took up again the random tramping in the dark unknown night; till it was two o'clock of a Sunday morning when at last I dropped my report-card in the train-guard box and climbed upstairs to the cot opposite "Davie," sleeping the silent, untroubled sleep of a babe.

I was barely settled in Gatun when the train-guard handed me one of those frequent typewritten orders calling for the arrest of some straggler or deserter from the marine camp of the Tenth Infantry. That very morning I had seen "the boss" of census days off on his vacation to the States—from which he might not return —and here I was coldly and peremptorily called upon to go forth and arrest and deliver to Camp Elliott on its hill

"Mac," the pride of the census, with a promise of $25 reward for the trouble. "Mac" desert? It was to laugh. But naturally after six weeks of unceasing repetition of that pink set of questions "Mac's" throat was a bit dry and he could scarcely be expected to return at once to the humdrum life of camp without spending a bit of that $5 a day in slaking a tropical thirst. Indeed I question whether any but the prudish will loudly blame "Mac" even because he spent it a bit too freely and brought up in Empire dispensary. Word of his presence there soon drifted down to the wily plain−clothes man of Empire district. But it was a hot noonday, the dispensary lies somewhat up hill, and the uniformless officer of the Zone metropolis is rather thickly built. Wherefore, stowing away this private bit of information under his hat, he told himself with a yawn, "Oh, I'll drag him in later in the day," and drifted down to a wide−open door on Railroad Avenue to spend a bit of the $25 reward in off−setting the heat. Meanwhile "Mac," feeling somewhat recovered from his financial extravagance, came sauntering out of the dispensary and, seeing his curly−headed friend strolling a beat not far away, naturally cried out, "Hello, Eck!" And what could Eck say, being a reputable Zone policeman, but:

"Why, hello, Mac! How they framin' up? Consider yourself pinched."

Which was lucky for "Mac." For Eck had once worn a marine hat over his own right eye and, he knew from melancholy experience that the $25 was no government generosity, but "Mac's" own involuntary contribution to his finding and delivery; so managed to slip most of it back into "Mac's" hands.

Long, long after, more than six weeks after in fact, I chanced to be in Bas Obispo with a half−hour to spare, and climbed to the flowered and many−roaded camp on its far−viewing hilltop that falls sheer away on the east into the canal. In one of the airy barracks I found Renson, cards in hand, clear−skinned and "fit" now, thanks to the regular life of this adult nursery, though his lost youth was gone for good. And "Mac"? Yes, I saw "Mac" too—or at least the back of his head and shoulders through the screen of the guard−house where Renson pointed him out to me as he was being locked up again after a day of shoveling sand.

The first days in Gatun called for little else than patrol duty, without fixed hours, interspersed with an occasional loaf on the second−story veranda of the police−station overlooking the giant locks; close at hand was the entrance to the canal, up which came slowly barges loaded with crushed stone from Porto Bello quarry twenty miles east along the coast or sand from Nombre de Dios, twice as distant, while further still, spread Limon Bay from which swept a never-ending breeze one could wipe dry on as on a towel. So long as he has in his pocket no typewritten report with the Inspector's scrawl across it, "For investigation and report," the plain-clothes man is virtually his own commander, with few duties beside trying to be in as many parts of his district at once as possible and the ubiquitous duty of "keeping in touch with headquarters." So I wandered and mingled with all the life of the vicinity, exactly as I should have done had I not been paid a salary to do so. By day one could watch the growth of the great locks, the gradual drowning of little green, new-made islands beneath the muddy still waters of Gatun Lake, tramp out along jungle-flanked country roads, through the Mindi hills, or down below the old railroad to where the cayucas that floated down the Chagres laden with fruit came to land on the ever advancing edge of the waters. With night things grew more compact. From twilight till after midnight I prowled in and out through New Gatun, spilled far and wide over its several hills, watching the antics of negroes, pausing to listen to their guitars and their boisterous merriment, with an eye and ear ever open for the unlawful. When I drifted into a saloon to see who might be spending the evening out, the bar-tender proved he had the advantage of me in acquaintance by crying: "Hello, Franck! What ye having?" and showing great solicitude that I get it. After which I took up the starlit tramp again, to run perhaps into some such perilous scene as on that third evening. A riot of contending voices rose from a building back in the center of a block, with now and then the sickening thump of a falling body. I approached noiselessly, likewise weaponless, peeped in and found—four negro bakers stripped to the waist industriously kneading to-morrow's bread and discussing in profoundest earnest the object of the Lord in creating mosquitoes. Beyond the native town, as an escape from all this, there was the back country road that wound for a mile through the fresh night and the droning jungle, yet instead of leading off into the wilderness of the interior swung around to American Gatun on its close-cropped hills.

I awoke one morning to find my name bulletined among those ordered to report for target test. A fine piece of luck was this for a man who had scarcely fired a shot since, aged ten, he brought down with an air-gun an occasional sparrow at three cents a head. We took the afternoon train to Mt. Hope on the edge of Colon and trooped away to a little plain behind "Monkey Hill," the last resting-place of many a "Zoner." The Cristobal Lieutenant, father of Z. P., was in charge, and here again was that same Z. P. absence of false dignity and the genuine good-fellowship that makes the success of your neighbor as pleasing as your own.

"Shall I borrow a gun, Lieutenant?" I asked when I found myself "on deck."

"Well, you'll have to use your own judgment as to that," replied the Lieutenant, busy pasting stickers over holes in the target.

The test was really very simple. All you had to do was to cling to one end of a No. 38 horse–pistol, point it at the bull's–eye of a target, hold it in that position until you had put five bullets into said bull's–eye, repeat that twice at growing distances, mortally wound ten times the image of a Martinique negro running back and forth across the field, and you had a perfect score. Only, simple as it was, none did it, not even old soldiers with two or three "hitches" in the army. So I had to be content with creeping in on the second page of a seven–page list of all the tested force from "the Chief" to the latest negro recruit.

The next evening I drifted into the police station to find a group of laborers from the adjoining camps awaiting me on the veranda bench, because the desk–man "didn't sabe their lingo." They proved upon examination to be two Italians and a Turk, and their story short, sad, but by no means unusual. Upon returning from work one of the Italians had found the lock hinges of his ponderously padlocked tin trunk hanging limp and screwless, and his pay–day roll of some $30 missing from the crown of a hat stuffed with a shirt securely packed away in the deepest corner thereof. The Turk was similarly unable to account for the absence of his $33 savings safely locked the night before inside a pasteboard suitcase; unless the fact that, thanks to some sort of surgical operation, one entire side of the grip now swung open like a barn–door might prove to have something to do with the case. The $33 had been, for further safety's sake, in Panamanian silver, suggesting a burglar with a wheelbarrow.

The mysterious detective work began at once. Without so much as putting on a false beard I repaired to the scene of the nefarious crime. It was the usual Zone type of laborers' barracks. A screened building of one huge room, it contained two double rows of three–tier "standee" canvas bunks on gas–pipes. Around the entire room, close under the sheet–iron roof, ran a wooden platform or shelf reached by a ladder and stacked high with the tin trunks, misshapen bundles, and pressed–paper suitcases containing the worldly possessions of the fifty or more workmen around the rough table below.

Theoretically not even an inmate thereof may enter a Zone labor– camp during working hours. Practically the West Indian janitors to whom is left the enforcement of this rule are

82

nothing if not fallible. In the course of the second day I unearthed a second Turk who, having chanced the morning before to climb to the baggage shelf for his razor and soap preparatory to welcoming a fellow countryman to the Isthmus, had been mildly startled to step on the shoulder–blade of a negro of given length and proportions lying prone behind the stacked–up impedimenta. The latter explained both his presence in a white labor–camp and his unconventional posture by asserting that he was the "mosquito man," and shortly thereafter went away from there without leaving either card or address.

By all my library training in detective work the next move obviously was to find what color of cigarette ashes the Turk smoked. Instead I blundered upon the absurdly simple notion of trying to locate the negro of given length and proportions. The real "mosquito man"—one of that dark band that spends its Zone years with a wire hook and a screened bucket gathering evidence against the defenseless mosquito for the sanitary department to gloat over—was found not to fit the model even in hue. Moreover, "mosquito men" are not accustomed to carry their devotion to duty to the point of crawling under trunks in their quest.

For a few days following, the hunt led me through all Gatun and vicinity. Now I found myself racing across the narrow plank bridges above the yawning gulf of the locks, with far below tiny men and toy trains, now in and out among the cathedral–like flying buttresses, under the giant arches past staring signs of "DANGER!" on every hand—as if one could not plainly hear its presence without the posting. I descended to the very floor of the locks, far below the earth, and tramped the long half–mile of the three flights between soaring concrete walls. Above me rose the great steel gates, standing ajar and giving one the impression of an opening in the Great Wall of China or of a sky–scraper about to be swung lightly aside. On them resounded the roar of the compressed– air riveters and all the way up the sheer faces, growing smaller and smaller as they neared the sky, were McClintic–Marshall men driving into place red–hot rivets, thrown at them viciously by negroes at the forges and glaring like comets' tails against the twilight void.

The chase sent me more than once stumbling away across rock– tumbled Gatun dam that squats its vast bulk where for long centuries, eighty–five feet below, was the village of Old Gatun with its proud church and its checkered history, where Morgan and Peruvian viceroys and "Forty–niners" were wont to pause from their arduous journeyings. They call it a dam. It is rather a range of hills, a part and portion of the highlands that, east and west, enclose the valley of the Chagres, its summit resembling the terminal yards of some great city. There was one day when I sought a negro brakeman attached to a given locomotive. I climbed to a yard–master's tower above the Spillway and the yard–master, taking up his powerful field–glasses, swept the horizon, or rather the dam, and discovered the engine for me as a mariner discovers an island at sea.

"Er—would you be kind enough to tell us where we can find this Gatun dam we've heard so much about?" asked a party of four tourists, half and half as to sex, who had been wandering about on it for an hour or so with puzzled expressions of countenance. They addressed themselves to a busy civil engineer in leather leggings and rolled up shirt sleeves.

"I'm sorry I haven't time to use the instrument," replied the engineer over his shoulder, while he wig–wagged his orders to his negro helpers scattered over the landscape, "but as nearly as I can tell with the naked eye, you are now standing in the exact center of it."

The result of all this sweating and sight–seeing was that some days later there was gathered in a young Barbadian who had been living for months in and about Gatun without any visible source of income whatever—not even a wife. The Turk and the camp janitor identified him as the culprit. But the primer lesson the police recruit learns is that it is one thing to believe a man guilty and quite another to convince a judge—the most skeptical being known to zoology—of that perfectly apparent fact. With the suspect behind bars, therefore, I continued my underground activities, with the result that when at length I took the train at New Gatun one morning for the court–room in Cristobal I loaded into a second–class coach six witnesses aggregating five nationalities, ready to testify among other things to the interesting little point that the defendant had a long prison record in Barbados.

When the echo of the black policeman's "Oye! Oye!" had died away and the little white–haired judge had taken his "bench," I made the discovery that I was present not in one, but in four capacities,—as arresting officer, complainant, interpreter, and to a large extent prosecuting attorney. To swear a Turk who spoke only Turkish through another Turk, who mangled a little Spanish, for a judge who would not recognize a non–American word from the voice of a steam–shovel, with a solemn "So Help Me God!" to clinch and strengthen it when the witness was a follower of the prophet of Medina—or nobody—was not without its possibilities of humor. The trial proceeded; the witnesses witnessed in their various tongues, the perspiring arresting officer reduced their statements to the common denominator of the judge's single tongue, and the smirking bullet—headed defendant was hopelessly buried under the evidence. Wherefore, when the shining black face of his lawyer, retained during the two minutes between the "Oye!" and the opening of the case, rose above the scene to purr:

"Your Honor, the prosecution has shown no case. I move the charge against my client be quashed."

I choked myself just in time to keep from gasping aloud, "Well, of all the nerve!" Never will I learn that the lawyer's profession admits lying on the same footing with truth in the defense of a culprit.

"Cause shown," mumbled the Judge without looking up from his writing, "defendant bound over for trial in the circuit court."

A week later, therefore, there was a similar scene a story higher in the same building. Here on Thursdays sits one of the three members of the Zone Supreme Court. Jury trial is rare on the Isthmus—which makes possibly for surer justice. This time there was all the machinery of court and I appeared only in my legal capacity. The judge, a man still young, with an astonishingly mobile face that changed at least once a minute from a furrowy scowl with great pouting lips to a smile so broad it startled, sat in state in the middle of three judicial arm—chairs, and the case proceeded. Within an hour the defendant was standing up, the cheery grin still on his black countenance, to be sentenced to two years and eight months in the Zone penitentiary at Culebra. A deaf man would have fancied he was being awarded some prize. One of the never—ending surprises on the Zone is the apparent indifference of negro prisoners whether they get years or go free. Even if they testify in their own behalf it is in a listless, detached way, as if the matter were of no importance anyway. But the glance they throw the innocent arresting officer as they pass out on their way to the barb—wire enclosure on the outskirts of the Zone capital tells another story. There are members of the Z. P. who sleep with a gun under their pillow because of that look or a muttered word. But even were I nervous I should have been little disturbed at the glare in this case, for it will probably be a long walk from Culebra penitentiary to where I am thirty—two months from that morning.

A holiday air brooded over all Gatun and the country—side. Workmen in freshly washed clothing lolled in the shade of labor—camps, black Britishers were gathering in flat meadows fitted for the national game of cricket, far and wide sounded the care-free laughter and chattering of negroes, while even within Gatun police station leisure and peace seemed almost in full possession.

The morning "touch" with headquarters over, therefore, I scrambled away across the silent yawning locks and the trainless and workless dam to the Spillway, over which already some overflow from the lake was escaping to the Caribbean. My friends "Dusty" and H—— had carried their canoe to the Chagres below, and before nine we were off down the river. It was a day that all the world north of the Tropic of Cancer could not equal; just the weather for a perfect "day off." A plain-clothes man, it is true, is not supposed to have days off. Some one might run away with the Administration Building on the edge of the Pacific and the telephone wires be buzzing for me—with the sad result that a few days later there would be posted in Zone police stations where all who turned the leaves might read:

> Special Order No. ....
> Having been found Guilty of charges of
> Neglect of Duty
> preferred against him by his commanding officer
> First-class Policeman No. 88
> is hereby fined $2.
>
> Chief of Division.

But shades of John Aspinwall! Should even a detective work on such a Sunday? Surely no criminal would—least of all a black one. Moreover these forest-walled banks were also part of my beat.

The sun was hot, yet the air of that ozone-rich quality for which Panama is famous. For headgear we had caps; and did not wear those, though barely a few puffy, snow-white clouds ventured out into the vast chartless sky all the brilliant day through. Then the river; who could describe this lower reach of the Chagres as it curves its seven deep and placid miles from where Uncle Sam releases it from custody, to the ocean. Its jungled banks were without a break, for the one or two clusters of thatch and reed huts along the way are but a part of the living vegetation. Now and then we had glimpses across the tree-tops of brilliant green jungle hills further inland, everywhere were huge splendid trees, the stack–shaped mango, the soldier–erect palm heavy, yet unburdened, with cocoanuts. Some fish resembling the porpoise rose here and there, back and forth above the shadows winged snow–white cranes so slender one wondered the sea breeze did not wreck them. Above all the quiet and peace and contentment of a perfect tropical day enfolded the landscape in a silence only occasionally disturbed by the cry of a passing bird. Once a gasoline launch deep–laden with Sunday–starched Americans, snorted by, bound likewise to Fort Lorenzo at the river's mouth; and we lay back in our soft, rumpled khaki and drowsily smiled our sympathy after them. When they had drawn on out of earshot life began to return to the banks and nature again took possession of the scene. Alligators abounded once on this lower Chagres, but they have grown scarce now, or shy, and though we sat with H——'s automatic rifle across our knees in turns we saw no more than a carcass or a skeleton on the bank at the foot of the sheer wall of impenetrable verdure.

Till at length the sea opened on our sight through the alley–way of jungle, and a broad inviting cocoanut grove nodded and beckoned on our left. Instead we paddled out across the sandbar to play with the surf of the Atlantic, but found it safer to return and glide across the little bay to the drowsy straw and tin village. Here—for the mouth of the Chagres like its source lies in a foreign land—a solitary Panamanian policeman in the familiar Arctic uniform enticed us toward the little thatched office, and house, and swinging hammock of the alcalde to register our names, and our business had we had any. So deep–rooted was the serenity of the place that even when "Dusty," in all Zone innocence, addressed the white–haired little mulatto as "hombre" he lost neither his dignity nor his temper.

The policeman and a brown boy of merry breed went with us up the grassy rise to the old fort. In its musty vaulted dungeons were still the massive, rust–corroded irons for feet, waist and neck of prisoners of the old brutal days; blind owls stared upon us; once the boy brought down with his honda, or slung–shot, one of the bats that circled uncannily above our heads. In dank corners were mounds of worthless powder; the bakery that once fed the miserable dungeon dwellers had crumbled in upon itself. Outside great trees straddled and split the massive stone walls that once commanded the entrance to the Chagres, jungle waved in undisputed possession in its earth–filled moat, even the old cannon and heaped up cannon–balls lay rust–eaten and dejected, like decrepit old men who have long since given up the struggle.

We came out on the nose of the fort bluff and had before and below us and underfoot all the old famous scene, for centuries the beginning of all trans–Isthmian travel,—the scalloped surf–washed shore with its dwindling palm groves curving away into the west, the Chagres pushing off into the jungled land. We descended to the beach of the outer bay and swam in the salt sea, and the policeman, scorning the launch party, squatted a long hour in the shade of a tree above in tropical patience. Then with "sour" oranges for thirst and nothing for hunger—for Lorenzo has no restaurant—we turned to paddle our way homeward up the Chagres, that bears the salt taste of the sea clear to the Spillway. Whence one verse only of a stanza by the late bard of the Isthmus struck a false note on our ears;

> Then go away if you have to,
> Then go away if you will!
> To again return you will always yearn
> While the lamp is burning still.
> You've drunk the Chagres water
> And the mango eaten free,
> And, strange though it seems,
> It will haunt your dreams
> This Land of the Cocoanut Tree.

No catastrophe had befallen during my absence. The same peaceful sunny Sunday reigned in Gatun; new–laundered laborers were still lolling in the shade of the camps, West Indians were still batting at interminable balls with their elongated paddles in the faint hope of deciding the national game before darkness settled down. Then twilight fell and I set off through the rambling town already boisterous with church services. Before the little sub–station a swarm of negroes was pounding tamborines and bawling lustily:

> Oh, yo mus' be a lover of de Lard
> Or yo cahn't go t' Heaven when yo di–ie.

Further on a lady who would have made ebony seem light–gray bowed over an organ, while a burly Jamaican blacker than the night outside stood in the vestments of the Church of England, telling his version of the case in a voice that echoed back from the town across the gully, as if he would drown out all rival sects and arguments by volume of sound. The meeting–house on the next corner was thronged with a singing multitude, tamborines scattered among them and all clapping hands to keep time, even to the pastor, who let the momentum carry on and on into verse after verse as if he had not the self–sacrifice to stop it, while outside in the warm night another crowd was gathered at the edge of the shadows gazing as at a vaudeville performance. How well–fitted are the various brands of Christianity to the particular likings of their "flocks." The strongest outward manifestation of the religion of the West Indian black is this boisterous singing. All over town were dusky throngs exercising their strong untrained voices "in de Lard's sarvice"; though the West Indian is not noted as being musical. Here a preacher wanting suddenly to emphasize a point or clinch an argument swung an arm like a college cheer leader and the entire congregation roared forth with him some well–known hymn that settled the question for all time.

I strolled on into darker High street. Suddenly on a veranda above there broke out a wild unearthly screaming. Two negroes were engaged in savage, sanguinary combat. Around them in the dim light thrown by a cheap tenement lamp I could make out their murderous weapons—machetes or great bars of iron—slashing wildly, while above the din rose screams and curses:

Yo——Badgyan, ah kill yo!

I sped stealthily yet swiftly up the long steps, drawing my No. 38 (for at last I had been issued one) as I ran and dashed into the heart of the turmoil swallowing my tendency to shout "Unhand him, villain!" and crying instead:

"Here, what the devil is going on here?"

Whereupon two negroes let fall at once two pine sticks and turned upon me their broad childish grins with:

"We only playin', sar. Playin' single–sticks which we larn to de army in Bahbaydos, sahgeant."

Thus I wandered on, in and out, till the night lost its youth and the last train from Colon had dumped its merry crowd at the station, then wound away along the still and deserted back road through the night–chirping jungle between the two surviving Gatuns. There was a spot behind the Division Engineer's hill that I rarely succeeded in passing without pausing to drink in the scene, a scallop in the hills where several trees stood out singly and alone against the myriad starlit sky, below and beyond the indistinct valleys and ravines from which came up out of the night the chorus of the jungle. Further on, in American Gatun there was a seat on the steps before a bungalow that offered more than a good view in both directions. A broad, U. S.–tamed ravine sank away in front, across which the Atlantic breeze wafted the distance–softened thrum of guitar, the tones of fifes and happy negro voices, while overhead feathery gray clouds as concealing as a dancer's gossamer hurried leisurely by across the brilliant face of the moon; to the right in a free space the Southern Cross, tilted a bit awry, gleamed as it has these untold centuries while ephemeral humans come and pass their brief way.

It was somewhere near here that Gatun's dry–season mosquito had his hiding–place. Rumor whispers of some such letter as the following received by the Colonel—not the blue–eyed czar at Culebra this time; for you must know there is another Colonel on the Zone every whit as indispensable in his sphere:

GATUN, ... 26, 1912.

Dear Colonel:—

I am writing to call your attention to a gross violation of Sanitary Ordinance No. 3621, to an apparent loop–hole in your otherwise excellent department. The circumstances are as follows;

On the evening of ... 24, as I was sitting at the roadside between Gatun and New Gatun (some 63 paces beyond house No. 226) there appeared a MOSQUITO, which buzzed openly and for some time about my ears. It was probably merely a male of the species, as it showed no tendency to bite; but a mosquito nevertheless. I trust you will take fitting measures to punish so bold and insolent a violation of the rules of your department.

I am, sir, very truly yours,

(Mrs.) HENRY PECK.

P. S. The mosquito may be easily recognized by a peculiarly triumphant, defiant note in his song,

I cannot personally vouch for the above, but if it was received any "Zoner" will assure you that prompt action was taken. It is well so. The French failed to dig the canal because they could not down the mosquito. Of course there was the champagne and the other things that come with it—later in the night. But after all it was the little songful mosquito that drove them in disgrace back across the Atlantic.

Still further on toward the hotel and a midnight lunch there was one house that was usually worth lingering before, though good music is rare on the Zone. Then there was the naughty poker game in bachelor quarters number—well, never mind that detail—to keep an ear on in case the pot grew large enough to make a worth–while violation of the law that would warrant the summoning of the mounted patrolman.

Meanwhile "cases" stacked up about me. Now one took me out the hard U. S. highway that, once out of sight of the last negro shanty, rambles erratically off like the reminiscences of an old man through the half–cleared, mostly uninhabited wilderness, rampant green with rooted life and almost noisy with the songs of birds. Eventually within a couple of hours it crossed Fox River with its little settlement and descended to Mt. Hope police station, where there is a 'phone with which to "get in touch" again and then a Mission rocker on the screened veranda where the breezes of the near–by Atlantic will have you well cooled off before you can catch the shuttle–train back to Gatun.

Or another led out across the lake by the old abandoned line that was the main line when first I saw Gatun. It drops down beyond the station and charges across the lake by a causeway that steam– shovels were already devouring, toward forsaken Bohio. Picking its way across the rotting spiles of culverts, it pushed on through the unpeopled jungle, all the old railroad gone, rails, ties, the very spikes torn up and carried away, while already the parrots screamed again in derision as if it were they who had driven out the hated civilization and taken possession again of their own. A few short months and the devouring jungle will have swallowed up even the place where it has been.

If it was only the little typewritten slip reporting the disappearance of a half–dozen jacks from the dam, every case called for full investigation. For days to come I might fight my way through the encircling wilderness by tunnels of vegetation to every native hut for miles around to see if by any chance the lost property could have rolled thither. More than once such a hunt brought me out on the water–tank knoll at the far end of the dam, overlooking miles of impenetrable jungle behind and above chanting with invisible life, to the right the filling lake stretching across to low blue ranges dimly outlined against the horizon and crowned by fantastic trees, and all Gatun and its immense works and workers below and before me.

Times were when duty called me into the squalid red-lighted district of Colon and kept me there till the last train was gone. Then there was nothing left but to pick my way through the night out along the P.R.R. tracks to shout in at the yard-master's window, "How soon y' got anything goin' up the line?" and, according to the answer, return to read an hour or two in Cristobal Y.M.C.A. or push on at once into the forest of box-cars to hunt out the lighted caboose. Night freights do not stop at Gatun, nor anywhere merely to let off a "gum-shoe." But just beyond New Gatun station is a grade that sets the negro fireman to sweating even at midnight and the big Mogul to straining every nerve and sinew, and I did not meet the engineer that could drag his long load by so swiftly but that one could easily swing off on the road that leads to the police station.

Even on the rare days when "cases" gave out there was generally something to while away the monotony. As, one morning an American widely known in Gatun was arrested on a warrant and, chatting merrily with his friend, Policeman ——, strolled over to the station. There his friend Corporal Macey subdued his broad Irish smile and ordered the deskman to "book him up." The latter was reaching for the keys to a cell when the American broke off his pleasant flow of conversation to remark;

"All right, Corporal, I'm going over to the house to get a few things and write a few letters. I'll be back inside of an hour."

Whereupon Corporal Macey, being a man of iron self-control, refrained from turning a double back sommersault and mildly called the prisoner's attention to a little point of Zone police rules he had overlooked.

If every other known form of amusement absolutely failed it was still the dry, or tourist season, and poured down from the States hordes of unconscious comedians, or investigators who rushed two whole days about the Isthmus, taking care not to get into any dirty places, and rushed home again to tell an eager public all about it. Sometimes the sight-seers came from the opposite end of the earth, a little band of South Americans in tongueless awe at the undreamed monster of work about them, yet struggling to keep their fancied despite of the "yanqui," to which the "yanqui" is so serenely indifferent.

Priests from this southland were especially numerous. The week never passed that a group of them might not be seen peering over the dizzy precipice of Gatun locks and crossing themselves ostentatiously as they turned away.

One does not, at least in a few months, feel the "sameness" of climate at Panama and "long again to see spring grow out of winter." Yet there is something, perhaps, in the popular belief that even northern energy evaporates in this tropical land. It is not exactly that; but certainly many a "Zoner" wakes up day by day with ambitious plans, and just drifts the day through with the fine weather. He fancies himself as strong and energetic as in the north, yet when the time comes for doing he is apt to say, "Oh, I guess I'll loaf here in the shade half an hour longer," and before he knows it another whole day is charged up against his meager credit column with Father Time.

There came the day early in April when the Inspector must go north on his forty–two days' vacation. I bade him bon voyage on board the 8:41 between the two Gatuns and soon afterward was throwing together my belongings and leaving "Davie" to enjoy his room alone. For Corporal Castillo was to be head of the subterranean department ad interim, and how could the digging of the canal continue with no detective in all the wilderness of morals between the Pacific and Culebra? Thus it was that the afternoon train bore me away to the southward. It was a tourist train. A New York steamer had docked that morning, and the first–class cars were packed with venturesome travelers in their stout campaign outfits in which to rough it—in the Tivoli and the sight–seeing motors— in their roof–like cork helmets and green veils for the terrible Panama heat—which is sometimes as bad as in northern New York.

The P.R.R. is one of the few railroads whose passengers may drop off for a stroll, let the train go on without them, and still take it to their destination. They have only to descend, as I did, at Gamboa cabin and wander down into the "cut," climb leisurely out to Bas Obispo, and chat with their acquaintances among the Marines lolling about the station until the trains puffs in from its shuttle–back excursion to Gorgona. The Zone landscape had lost much of its charm. For days past jungle fires had been sweeping over it, doing the larger growths small harm but leaving little of the greenness and rank clinging life of other seasons. Everywhere were fires along the way, even in the towns. For quartermasters— to the rage of Zone house–wives were sending up in clouds of smoke the grass and bushes that quickly turn to breeding–places of mosquitoes and disease with the first rains. Night closed down as we emerged from Miraflores tunnel; soon we swung around toward the houses, row upon row and all alight, climbed the lower slope of Ancon hill, and at seven I descended in familiar, cab–crowded, bawling Panama.

CHAPTER VII

It might be worth the ink to say a word about socialism on the Canal Zone. To begin with, there isn't any of course. No man would dream of looking for socialism in an undertaking set in motion by the Republican party and kept on the move by the regular army. But there are a number of little points in the management of this private government strip of earth that savors more or less faintly of the Socialist's program, and the Zone offers perhaps as good a chance as we shall ever have to study some phases of those theories in practice.

Few of us now deny the Socialist's main criticisms of existing society; most of us question his remedies. Some of us go so far as to feel a sneaking curiosity to see railroads and similar purely public utilities government–owned, just to find how it would work. Down on the Canal Zone they have a sort of modified socialism where one can watch much of this under a Bell jar. There one quickly discovers that a locomotive with the brief and sufficient information "U.S." on her tender flanks—or more properly the flanks of her tender—gives one a swelling of the chest no other combination of letters could inspire. Thus far, too, theory seems to work well. The service could hardly be better, and recalling that under the old private system the fare for the forty–seven miles across the Isthmus was $25 with a charge of ten cents for every pound of baggage, the $2.40 of today does not seem particularly exorbitant.

The official machinery of this private government strip also seems to run like clockwork. To be sure the wheels even of a clock grind a bit with friction at times, but the clock goes on keeping time for all that. The Canal Zone is the best governed district in the United States. It is worth any American's time and sea–sickness to run down there, if only to assure himself that Americans really can govern; until he does he will not have a very clear notion of just what good American government means.

But before we go any further be it noted that the socialism of the Canal Zone is under a benevolent despot, an Omnipotent, Omniscient, Omnipresent ruler; which is perhaps the one way socialism would work, at least in the present stage of human progress. The three

Omnis are combined in an inconspicuous, white– haired American popularly known on the Zone as "the Colonel"—so popularly in fact that an attempt to replace him would probably "start something" among all classes and races of "Zoners." That he is omnipotent—on the Zone—not many will deny; a few have questioned—and landed in the States a week later much less joyous but far wiser. Omniscient—well they have even Chinese secret– service men on the Isthmus, and soldiers and marines not infrequently go out in civilian clothes under sealed orders; to say nothing of "the Colonel's private gum–shoe" and probably a lot of other underground sources of information neither you nor I shall ever hear of. But you must get used to spies under socialism, you know, until we all wear one of Saint Peter's halos. Look at the elaborate system of the Incas, even with their docile and uninitiative subjects. In the matter of Omnipresence; it would be pretty hard to find a hole on the Canal Zone where you could pull off a stunt of any length or importance without the I.C.C. having a weather–eye on you. When it comes to the no less indispensable ingredient of benevolence one glimpse of those mild blue eyes would probably reassure you in that point, even without the pleasure of watching the despot sit in judgment on his subjects in his castle office on Sunday mornings like old Saint Louis under his oak—though with a tin of cigarettes beside him that old Louis had to worry along without.

This all–powerful government insists on and enforces many of the things which Americans as a whole stand for,—Sunday closing, suppression of resorts, forbidding of gambling. But the Zone is no test whether these laws could be genuinely enforced in a whole nation. For down there Panama and Colon serve as a sort of safety– valve, where a man can run down in an hour or so on mileage or monthly pass and blow off steam; get rid of the bad internal vapors that might cause explosion in a ventless society. This we should not lose sight of when we boast that there are few crimes and no real resorts on the Zone. "The Colonel" himself will tell you there is no gambling. Yet it is curious how many of the weekly prizes of the Panama lottery find their way into the pockets of American canal builders, and in any Zone gathering of whatever hour—or sex!—you are almost certain to hear flitting back and forth mysterious whispers of "—have a 6 and a 4 this week."

The Zone system is work–coupons for all; much as the Socialist would have it. Only the legitimate members of the community—the workers—can live in it—long. You should see the nonchalant way a clerk at the government's Tivoli hotel charges a tourist a quarter for a cigar the government sells for six cents in its commissaries. Mere money does not rank high in Zone society. It's the labor–coupon that counts. They sell cigarettes at the Y.M.C.A.; you are in that state where you would give your ticket home for a smoke. Yet when you throw down good gold or silver, black Sam behind the showcase looks up at you with that pitying cold eye kept in stock for new–comers, and says wearily:

"Cahn't take no money heah, boss."

That surely is a sort of socialism where a slip of paper showing merely that you have done your appointed task gets you the same meal wherever you may drop in, a total stranger, yet without being identified, without a word from any one, but merely thrusting your coupon–book at the yellow West Indian at the door as you enter that he may snatch out so many minutes of labor. Drop in anywhere there is a vacant bed and you are perfectly at home. There is the shower–bath, the ice–water, the veranda rocker—you knew exactly what was coming to you, just what kind of bed, just what vegetables you would be served at dinner. It reminds one of the Inca system of providing a home for every citizen, and tambos along the way if he must travel.

But it IS the same meal. That is just the point. There is where you begin to furrow your brow and look more closely at this splendid system, and fall to wondering if that public kitchen of socialism would not become in time an awful bore. There are some things in which we want variety and originality and above all personality. A meal is a meal, I suppose, as a cat is a cat; yet there are many subtle little things that make the same things distinctly different. When it comes to dinner you want a rosy fat German or a bulky French madame putting thought and pride and attention into it; which they will do only if they get good coin of the realm or similar material emolument out of it in proportion. No one will ever fancy he has a "mission" to serve good meals—to the public.

In the I.C.C. hotels we have a government steward who draws a good salary and wears a nice white collar. But though he is sometimes a bit different, and succeeds in making his hotel so, it is only in degree. He is not a great frequenter of the dining–room; at times one wonders just what his activities are. Certainly it is not the planning of meals, for the I.C.C. menu is as fixed and automatic as if it had been taken from a stone slab in the pyramids. A poor meal neither turns his hair white nor cuts down his income. Frequently, especially if he is English and certainly if he has been a ship's steward, the negro waiters seem to run his establishment without interference. Dinner hours, for example, are from 11 to 1. But beware the glare of the waiter at whose table you sit down at 12:50. He slams cold rubbish at you from the discard and snatches it away again before you have time to find you can't eat it. You have your choice of enduring this maltreatment or of unostentatiously slipping him a coin and a hint to go cook you the best he can himself. For you know that as the closing hour approaches the cooks will not have their private plans interfered with by accepting your order. Here again is where the fat German or the French madame is needed—with an ox−goad.

In other words the tip system invented by Pharaoh and vitiated by quick−rich Americans rages as fiercely in government hotels on the Zone as in any "lobster palace" bordering Broadway—worse, for here the non−tipper has no living being to advocate his cause. All food is government property. Yet I have sat down opposite a man who gave the government at the door a work−coupon identical with mine, but who furthermore dropped into the waiter's hand "35 cents spig"—which is half as bad as to do it in U.S. currency—and while I was gazing tearfully at a misshapen lump of vacunal gristle there was set before him, steaming hot from the government kitchen, a porterhouse steak which a dollar bill would not have brought him within scenting distance of in New York. Do not blame the waiter. If he does not slip an occasional coin to the cook he will invariably draw the gristle, and even occasional coins do not grow on his waist band. It would be as absurd to charge it to the cook. He probably has a large family to support, as he would have under socialism. There runs this story on the Zone, vouched for by several:

A "Zoner" called an I.C.C. steward and complained that his waiter did not serve him reasonably:

"Well," sneered the steward, "I guess you didn't come across?"

"Come across! Why, damn you, I suppose you're getting your rake− off too?"

"I certainly am," replied the steward; "What do you think I'm down here for, me health?"

Surely we can't blame it all to the steward, or to any other individual. Lay it rather to human nature, that stumbling−block of so many varnished and upholstered systems.

I hope I am not giving the impression that I.C.C. hotels are unendurable. "Stay home"—which on the Zone means always eat at the same hotel table—subsidize your waiter and you do moderately well. But to move thither and yon, as any plain−clothes man must, is unfortunate. The only difference then is that the next is worse than the last. Whatever their convictions upon arrival, almost all Americans have come down to paying their waiter the regular blackmail of a dollar a month and setting it down as one of the unavoidable evils of life. One or two I knew who insisted on sticking to "principles," and they grew leaner and lanker day by day.

Because of these things many an American employee will be found eating in private restaurants of the ubiquitous Chinaman or the occasional Spaniard, though here he must often pay in cash instead of in futures on his labor—which are so much cheaper the world over. It is sad enough to dine on the same old identical round for months. But how if you were one of those who blew in on the heels of the last Frenchman and have been eating it ever since? By this time even rat–tails would be a welcome change—and with genuine socialism there would not even be that escape. It is said to be this hotel problem as much as the perpetual spring–time of the Zone that so frequently reduces—with the open connivance of the government—a building housing forty–eight quiet, harmless bachelors to a four–family residence housing eight and gradually upwards; that wreaks such matrimonious havoc among the white– frocked stenographers who come down to type and remain to cook.

Besides the hotel there is the P.R.R. commissary, the government department stores. It is likewise laundry, bakery, ice–factory; it makes ice–cream, roasts coffee, sends out refrigerator–cars and a morning supply train to bring your orders right to your door—oh, yes, it strongly resembles what Bellamy dreamed years ago. Only, as in the case of the hotel, there seems to be a fly or two in the amber.

The laundry is tolerable—fancy turning your soiled linen over to a railroad company—all machine done of course, as everything would be under socialism, and no come–back for the garment that is not hardy enough of constitution to stand the system. In the stores is little or no shoddy material; in general the stock is the best available. If a biscuit or a bolt of khaki is better made in England than in the United States the commissary stocks with English goods, which is unexpected broad–mindedness for government management. But while prices are lower than in Panama or Colon they are every whit as high as in American stores; and most of us know something of the exorbitant profit our private merchants exact, particularly on manufactured goods. The government claims to run the commissary only to cover cost. Either that is a crude government joke or there is a colored gentleman esconced in the coal–bin. Moreover if the commissary hasn't the stuff you want you had better give up wanting, for it has no object in laying in a supply of it just to oblige customers. Its clerks work in the most languid, unexcited manner. They have no object whatever in holding your trade, and you can wait until they are quite ready to serve you, or go home without. True, most of them are merely negroes, and the few Americans at the head of departments are chiefly provincial little fellows from small towns whose notions of business are rather those of Podunk, Mass., than of New York. But lolling about the commissary a half−hour hoping to buy a box of matches, one cannot shake off the conviction that it is the system more than the clerks. Poets and novelists and politicians may work for "glory," but no man is going to show calico and fit slippers for such remuneration.

Nor are all the old evils of the competitive method banished from the Zone. In the Canal Record, the government organ, the government commissary advertised a sale of excellent $7 rain−coats at $1 each. The "Record"! It is like reading it in the Bible. Witness the rush of bargain hunters, who, it proves, are by no means of one gender. Yet those splendid rain−coats, as manager, clerks, and even negro sweepers well knew and could not refrain from snickering to themselves at thought of, were just as rain− proof as a poor grade of cheese−cloth. I do not speak from hear− say for I was numbered among the bargain hunters—"recruits" are the natural victims, and there arrive enough of them each year to get rid of worthless stock. Ten minutes after making the purchase I set out to walk to Corozal through the first mild shower of the rainy season—and arrived there I went and laid the bargain gently in the waste−basket of Corozal police station.

Thus does the government sink to the petty rascalities of shop− keepers. Even a government manager on a fixed salary—in work− coupons—will descend to these tricks of the trade to keep out of the clutches of the auditor, or to make a "good record." The socialist's answer perhaps would be that under their system government factories would make only perfect goods. But won't the factory superintendent also be anxious to make a "record"? And even government stock will deteriorate on the shelves.

All small things, to be sure; but it is the sum of small things that make up that great complex thing—Life. Few of us would object to living in that ideal dream world. But could it ever be? I have anxiously asked this question and hinted at these little weaknesses suggested by Zone experiences to several Zone socialists—who are not hard to find. They merely answer that these things have nothing to do with the case. But not one of them ever went so far as to demonstrate; and though I was born a long way north of Missouri I once passed through a corner of the state.

As to the other side of the ledger,—equal pay for all, nowhere is man further from socialism than on the Canal Zone. Caste lines are as sharply drawn as in India, which should not be unexpected in an enterprise largely in charge of graduates of our chief training– school for caste. The Brahmins are the "gold" employees, white American citizens with all the advantages and privileges thereto appertaining. But—and herein we out–Hindu the Hindus—the Brahmin caste itself is divided and subdivided into infinitesimal gradations. Every rank and shade of man has a different salary, and exactly in accordance with that salary is he housed, furnished, and treated down to the least item,—number of electric lights, candle–power, style of bed, size of bookcase. His Brahmin highness, "the Colonel," has a palace, relatively, and all that goes with it. The high priests, the members of the Isthmian Canal Commission, have less regal palaces. Heads of the big departments have merely palatial residences. Bosses live in well–furnished dwellings, conductors are assigned a furnished house—or quarter of a house. Policemen, artisans, and the common garden variety of bachelors have a good place to sleep. It is doubtful, to be sure, whether one–fourth of the "Zoners" of any class ever lived as well before or since. The shovelman's wife who gives five–o'clock teas and keeps two servants will find life different when the canal is opened and she moves back to the smoky little factory cottage and learns again to do her own washing.

At work, "on the job" there is a genuine American freedom of wear– what–you–please and a general habit of going where you choose in working clothes. That is one of the incomprehensible Zone things to the little veneered Panamanian. He cannot rid himself of his racial conviction that a man in an old khaki jacket who is building a canal must be of inferior clay to a hotel loafer in a frock coat and a tall hat. The real "Spig" could never do any real work for fear of soiling his clothes. He cannot get used to the plain, brusk American type without embroidery, who just does things in his blunt, efficient way without wasting time on little exterior courtesies. None of these childish countries is man enough to see through the rough surface. Even with seven years of American example about him the Panamanian has not yet grasped the divinity of labor. Perhaps he will eons hence when he has grown nearer true civilization.

But among Americans off the job reminiscences of East India flock in again. D, who is a quartermaster at $225, may be on "How–are– you–old–man?" terms with G, who is a station agent and draws $175. But Mrs. D never thinks of calling on Mrs. G socially. H and J, who are engineer and cranemen respectively on the same steam– shovel, are probably "Hank" and "Jim" to each other, but Mrs. H would be horrified to find herself at the same dance with Mrs. J. Mrs. X, whose husband is a foreman at $165, and whose dining table is a full six inches longer and whose ice–box will hold one more cold–storage chicken, would not think of sitting in at bridge with Mrs. Y, whose husband gets $150. As for being black, or any tint but pure "white"! Even an Englishman, though he may eat in the same hotel if his skin is not too tanned, is accepted on staring suffrance. As for the man whose skin is a bit dull, he might sit on the steps of an I. C. C. hotel with dollars dribbling out of his pockets until he starved to death—and he would be duly buried in the particular grave to which his color entitled him. A real American place is the Zone, with outward democracy and inward caste, an unenthusiastic and afraid–to–break–the–conventions place in play, and the opposite at work.

Yet with it all it is a good place in which to live. There you have always summer, jungled hills to look on by day and moonlight, and to roam in on Sunday—unless you are a policeman seven days a week. It is possible that perpetual summer would soon breed quite a different type of American. The Isthmus is nearly always in boyish—or girlish—good temper. Zone women and girls are noted for plump figures and care–free faces. And there is a contentment that is more than climatic. There are no hard times on the Zone, no hurried, worried faces, no famished, wolfish eyes. The "Zoner" has his little troubles of course,—the servant problem, for instance, for the Jamaican housemaid is a thorn in any side. Now and then we hear some one wailing, "Oh, it gets so—tiresome! Everybody's shoveling dirt or talking about the other fellow." But he knows it isn't strictly true when he says it and that he is kicking chiefly to keep in practice. Every one is free from worries as to job, pay, house, provisions, and even hospital fees, and the smoothness of it all, perhaps, gets on his nerves at times. I question whether "the Colonel" himself loses much sleep when a chunk of the hill that bears up his residence lets go and pitches into the canal. It sets one to musing at times whether the rock–bound system of the Incas was not best after all,—a place for every man and every man in his place, each his allotted work, which he was fully able to do and getting Hail Columbia if he failed to do it.

Which brings up the question of results in labor under the pseudo– socialist Zone system. Most American employees work steadily and take their work seriously. It is as if each were individually proud of being one of the chosen people and builders of the greatest work of modern times. Yet the far–famed "American rush" is not especially prevalent.

The Zone point of view seems to be that no shoveling is so important, even that of digging a ditch half the ships of the world are waiting to cross, that a man should bring upon himself a premature funeral. The common laborers, non–Americans, almost dawdle. There are no contractor's Irish straw–bosses to keep them on the move. The answer to the Socialist's scheme of having the government run all big building enterprises is to go out and watch any city street gang for an hour.

The bringing together into close contact of Americans from every section of our broad land is tending to make a new amalgamated type. Even New Englanders grow almost human here among their broader–minded fellow–countrymen. Any northerner can say "nigger" as glibly as a Carolinian, and growl if one of them steps on his shadow. It is not easy to say just how much effect all this will have when the canal is done and this handful of amalgamated and humanized Americans is sprinkled back over all the States as a leaven to the whole. They tell on the Zone of a man from Maine who sat four high–school years on the same bench with two negro boys, and returning home after three years on the Isthmus was so horrified to find one of those boys an alderman that he packed his traps and moved to Alabama, "where a nigger IS a nigger"—and if there isn't the "makings" of a story in that I 'll leave it to the postmaster of Miraflores.

CHAPTER VIII

"There is much in this police business," said "the Captain," with his slow, deliberate enunciation, "that must lead to a blank wall. Out of ten cases to investigate it is quite possible nine will result in nothing. This percentage could not of course be true of a thousand cases and a man's services still be considered satisfactory. But of ten it is quite possible. As for knowing HOW to do detective work, all I bring to the department myself is some ordinary common sense and a little knowledge of human nature, and with these I try to work things out as best I can. This peeping– through–the–key–hole police work I know nothing whatever about, and don't want to. Nor do I expect a man to."

I had been discussing with "the Captain" my dissatisfaction at my failure to "get results" in an important case. A few weeks on the force had changed many a preconceived notion of police life. It had gradually become evident, for instance, that the profession of detective is adventurous, absorbing, heart–stopping chiefly between the covers of popular fiction; that real detective work, like almost any other vocation, is made up largely of the little unimportant every–day details, with only a rare assignment bulking above the mass. As "the Captain" said, it was just plain every–day work carried on by the application of ordinary common sense. Such best–seller artifices as disguise were absurd. Not only would disguise in all but the rarest cases be impossible, but useless. The A–B–C of plain–clothes work is to learn to know a man by his face rather than by his clothing—and at the outset one will be astonished to find how much he has hitherto been depending on the latter. It must be the same with criminals, too, unless your criminal is an amateur or a fool, in which event you will "land" him without the trouble of disguising. A detective furthermore should not be a handsome man or a man of striking appearance in any way; the ideal plain–clothes man is the little insignificant snipe whom even the ladies will not notice.

Since April tenth I had been settled in notorious House 111, Ancon, a sort of frontiersman resort or smugglers' retreat—had there been anything to smuggle—where to have fallen through the veranda screening would have been to fall into a foreign land. As pay–day approached there came the duty of standing a half–hour at the station gate before the departure of each train to watch and discuss with the ponderous, smiling, dark–skinned chief of Panama's plain–clothes squad, or with a vigilante the suspicious characters and known crooks of all colors going out along the line. On the twelfth, thirteenth and fourteenth the I. C. C. pay– car, that bank on wheels guarded by a squad of Z. P., sprinkled its half–million a day along the Zone. Then plain–clothes duty was not merely to scan the embarking passengers but to ride out with each train to one of the busy towns. There scores upon scores of soil–smeared workmen swarmed over all the landscape with long paper–wrapped rolls of Panamanian silver in their hands, while flashily dressed touts and crooks of both sexes drifted out from Panama with every train to worm their insidious way into wherever the scent of coin promised another month free from labor. To add to those crowded times the chief dissipation of the West Indian during the few days following pay–day that his earnings last is to ride aimlessly and joyously back and forth on the trains.

There is one advantage, though some policemen call it by quite the opposite name, in being stationed at Ancon. When crime takes a holiday and do–nothing threatens tropical dementia, or a man tires of his native land and people a short stroll down the asphalt takes him into the city of Panama. Barely across the street where his badge becomes mere metal, and he must take care not to arrest absent–mindedly the first violator of Zone laws—whom he is sure to come upon within the first block—he notes that the English tongue has suddenly almost disappeared. On every hand, lightly sprinkled with many other dialects, sounds Spanish, the slovenly Spanish of Panama in which bueno is "hueno" and calle is "caye." As he swings languidly to the right into Avenida Central he grows gradually aware that there has settled down about him a cold indifference, an atmosphere quite different from that on his own side of the line. Those he addresses in the tongue of the land reply to his questions with their customary gestures and fixed phrases of courtesy. But no more; and a cold dead silence falls sharply upon the last word, and at times, if the experience be comparatively new, there seems to hover in the air something that reminds him that way back fifty–six years ago there was a "massacre" of Americans in Panama city. For the Panamanian has little love for the United States or its people; which is the customary thanks any man or nation gets for lifting a dirty half–breed gamin from the gutter.

Off in the vortex of the city lolls Panama's public market, where Chinamen are the chief sellers and flies the chief consumers. Myriads of fruits in every stage of development and disintegration, haggled bits of meat, the hundred sights and sounds and smells one hurries past suggest that Panama may even have outdone Central America before Uncle Sam came with his garbage–cans and his switch. Further on, down at the old harbor, lingers a hint of the picturesqueness of Panama in pre–canal days. Clumsy boats, empty, or deep–laden with fruit from, or freight to, the several islands that sprinkle the bay, splash and bump against the little cement wharf. Aged wooden "windjammers" doze at their moorings, everywhere are jabbering natives with that shifty half– cast eye and frequent evidence of deep–rooted disease. Almost every known race mingles in Panama city, even to Chinese coolies in their umbrella hats and rolled up cotton trousers, delving in rich market gardens on the edges of the town or dog–trotting through the streets under two baskets dancing on the ends of a bamboo pole, till one fancies oneself at times in Singapore or Shanghai. The black Zone laborer, too, often prefers to live in Panama for the greater freedom it affords—there he doesn't have to clean his sink so often, marry his "wife," or banish his chickens from the bedroom. Policemen with their clubs swarm everywhere, for no particular reason than that the little republic is forbidden to play at army, and with the presidential election approaching political henchmen must be kept good–humored. Not a few of these officers are West Indians who speak not a word of Spanish—nor any other tongue, strictly speaking.

Rubber–tired carriages roll constantly by along Uncle Sam's macadam, amid the jingling of their musical bells. Every one takes a carriage in Panama. Any man can afford ten cents even if he has no expense account; besides he runs no risk of being overcharged, which is a greater advantage than the cost. All this may be different when Panama's electric line, all the way from Balboa docks to Las Sabanas, is opened—but that's another year. Meanwhile the lolling in carriages comes to be quite second nature.

But like any tropical Spanish town Panama seethes only by night, especially Saturday and Sunday nights when the paternal Zone government allows its children to spend the evening in town. Then frequent trains, unknown during the week, begin with the setting of the sun to disgorge Americans of all grades and sizes through the clicking turnstiles into the arms of gesticulating hackmen, some to squirm away afoot between the carriages, all to be swallowed up within ten minutes in the great sea of "colored" people. So that, large as may be each train–load, white American faces are so rare on Panama streets that one involuntarily glances at each that passes in the throng.

It is the "gum–shoe's" duty to know and be unknown in as many places as possible. Wherefore on such nights, whatever his choice, he drifts early down by the "Normandie" and on into the "Pana– zone" to see who is out, and why. In the latter emporium he adds a bottle of beer to his expense account, endures for a few moments the bawling above the scream of the piano of two Americans of Palestinian antecedents, admires some local hero, like "Baldy" for instance, who is credited with doing what Napoleon could not do, and floats on, perhaps to screw up his courage and venture into the thinly–clad Teatro Apolo. He who knows where to look, or was born under a lucky star, may even see on these merry evenings a big Marine from Bas Obispo or a burly soldier of the Tenth howling some joyful song with six or seven little "Spig" policemen climbing about on his frame. At such times everything but real blood, flows in Panama. Her history runs that way. On the day she won her independence from Spain it is said the General in Chief cut his finger on a wine glass. The day she won it from Colombia there was a Chinaman killed—but every one agrees that was due to the celestial's criminal carelessness.

Down at the quieter end of the city are "Las Bovedas," that curving sea–wall Phillip of Spain tried to make out from his palace walls, as many another, regal and otherwise, has strained his eyes in vain to see where his good coin has gone. But the walls are there all right, though Phillip never saw them; crumbling a bit, yet still a sturdy barrier to the sea. A broad cement and grass promenade runs atop, wide as an American street. Thirty or forty feet below the low parapet sounds the deep, time– mellowed voice of the Pacific, as there rolls higher and higher up the rock ledges that great tide so different from the scarcely noticeable one at Colon. The summer breeze never dies down, never grows boisterous. On the landward side Panama lies mumbling to itself, down in the hollow between squats Chiriqui prison with its American warden, once a Zone policeman; while in the round stone watch–towers on the curving parapets lean prison guards with fixed bayonets and incessantly blow the shrill tin whistles that is the universal Latin–American artifice for keeping policemen awake. On the way back to the city the elite—or befriended—may drop in at the University Club at the end of the wall for a cooling libation.

On Sunday night comes the band concert in the palm–ringed Cathedral Plaza. There is one on Thursday, too, in Plaza Santa Ana, but that is packed with all colors and considered "rather vulgah." In the square by the cathedral the aggregate color is far lighter. Pure African blood hangs chiefly in the outskirts. Then the haughty aristocrats of Panama, proud of their own individual shade of color, may be seen in the same promenade with American ladies—even a garrison widow or two—from out along the line. Panamanian girls gaudily dressed and suggesting to the nostrils perambulating drug–stores shuttle back and forth with their perfumed dandies. Above the throng pass the heads and shoulders of unemotional, self–possessed Americans, erect and soldierly. Sergeant Jack of Ancon station was sure to be there in his faultless civilian garb, a figure neat but not gaudy; and even busy Lieutenant Long was known to break away from his stacked–up duties and his black stenographer and come to overtop all else in the square save the palm–trees whispering together in the evening breeze between the numbers.

There is no favoritism in Zone police work. Every crime reported receives full investigation, be it only a Greek laborer losing a pair of trousers or—

There was the case that fell to me early in May, for instance. A box billed from New York to Peru had been broken open on Balboa dock and—one bottle of cognac stolen. Unfortunately the matter was turned over to me so long after the perpetration of the dastardly crime that the possible culprits among the dock hands had wholly recovered from the probable consumption of the evidence. But I succeeded in gathering material for a splendid typewritten report of all I had not been able to unearth, to file away among other priceless headquarters' archives.

Not that the Z. P. has not its big jobs. The force to a man distinctly remembers that absorbing two months between the escape of wild black Felix Paul and the day they dragged him back into the penitentiary. No less fresh in memory are the expeditions against Maurice Pelote, or Francois Barduc, the murderer of Miraflores. All Martinique negroes, be it noted; and of all things on this earth, including greased pigs, the hardest to catch is a Martinique criminal. After all, four or five murders on the Zone in three years is no startling record in such a swarm of nationalities.

Cases large and small which it would be neither of interest nor politic to detail poured in during the following weeks. Among them was the counterfeit case unearthed by some Shylock Holmes on the Panamanian force, that called for a long perspiring hunt for the "plant" in odd corners of the Zone. Then there was—, an ex–Z. P. who lost his three years' savings on the train, for which reason I shadowed a well–known American—for it is a Z. P. rule that no one is above suspicion—about Panama afoot and in carriages nearly all night, in true dime–novel fashion. There was the day that I was given a dangerous convict to deliver at Culebra Penitentiary. The criminal was about three feet long, jet black, his worldly possessions comprising two more or less garments, one reaching as far down as his knees and the other as far up as the base of his neck. He had long been a familiar sight to "Zoners" among the swarm of bootblacks that infest the corner near the P. R. R. station. He claimed to be eleven, and looked it. But having already served time for burglary and horse–stealing, his conviction for stealing a gold necklace from a negro washerwoman of San Miguel left the Chief Justice no choice but to send him to meditate a half–year at Culebra. There is no reform school on the Zone. The few American minors who have been found guilty of misdoing have been banished to their native land. When the deputy warden had sufficiently recovered from the shock brought upon him by the sight of his new charge to give me a receipt for him, I raced for the noon train back to the city.

Thereon I sat down beside Pol—First–Class Policeman X——, surprised to find him off duty and in civilian clothes. There was a dreamy, far–away look in his eyes, and not until the train was racing past Rio Grande reservoir did he turn to confide to me the following extraordinary occurrence:

"Last night I dreamed old Judge———had my father and my mother up before him. On the stand he asked my mother her age—and the funny part of it is my mother has been dead over ten years. She turned around and wrote on the wall with a piece of chalk '1859,' the year she was born. Then my father was called and he wrote '1853.' That's all there was to the dream. But take it from me I know what it means. Now just add 'em together, and multiply by five—because I could see five people in the court-room—divide by two—father and mother—and I get—," he drew out a crumpled "arrest" form covered with penciled figures, "—9280. And there—" his voice dropped low, "—is your winning number for next Sunday."

So certain was this, that First-Class X——had bribed another policeman to take his eight-hour shift, dressed in his vacation best, bought a ticket to Panama and return, with real money at tourist prices, and would spend the blazing afternoon seeking among the scores of vendors in the city for lottery ticket 9280. And if he did not find it there he certainly paid his fare all the way to Colon and back to continue his search. I believe he at length found and acquired the whole ticket, for the customary sum of $2.50. But there must have been a slip in the arithmetic, or mother's chalk; for the winning number that Sunday was 8895.

Frequent as are these melancholy errors, scores of "Zoners" cling faithfully to their arithmetical superstitions. Many a man spends his recreation hours working out the winning numbers by some secret recipe of his own. There are men on the Z. P. who, if you can get them started on the subject of lottery tickets, will keep it up until you run away, showing you the infallibility of their various systems, believing the drawing to be honest, yet oblivious to the fact that both the one and the other cannot be true. Dreams are held in special favor. It is probably safe to assert that one- half the numbers over 1,000 and under 10,000 that appear in Zone dreams are snapped up next day in lottery tickets. Many have systems of figuring out the all-important number from the figures on engines and cars. More than one Zone housewife has slipped into the kitchen to find the roast burning and her West Indian cook hiding hastily behind her ample skirt a long list of the figures on every freight-car that has passed that morning, from which by some Antillian miscalculation and the murmuring of certain invocations she was to find the magic number that would bring her cooking days to an end.

Yet there is sometimes method in their madness. Did not "Joe" who slept in the next room to me at Gatun "hit Duque for two pieces"— which is to say he had $3,000 to sprinkle along with his police salary? Yet personally the only really appealing "system" was that of Cristobal. Upon his arrival on the Isthmus four years ago he picked out a number at random, took out a yearly subscription to it, and thought no more about it than one does of a newspaper delivered at the door each morning—until one Monday during this month of May, after he had squandered something over $500, on worthless bits of paper, he strolled into the lottery office and was handed an inconspicuous little bag containing $7,500 in yellow gold.

Like all Z. P. "rookies" (recruits) I had been warned early to beware the "sympathy dodge." But experience is the only real teacher. One afternoon I bestraddled a crazy, stilt–legged Jamaican horse to go out into the bush beyond the Panama line to fetch and deliver a citizen of that sovereign republic who was wanted on the Zone for horse–stealing. At the town of Sabanas, where those Panamanians who have bagged the most loot since American occupation have their "summer" homes,—giddy, brick–painted monstrosities among the great trees, deep green foliage and brilliant flower–beds (pause a moment and think of brilliant red houses in the tropics; it will make you better acquainted with the "Spig") I dropped in at the police station for ice–water and information. I found it in charge of a negro policeman who knew nothing, and had forgotten that. When, therefore, it also chanced that an officer of the Society for the Prevention of Cruelty to Animals stopped before the gate with a coachman of Panama, it fell upon me to assume command. The horse was the usual emaciated rat of an animal indigenous to Panama City. When overhauled, the driver was beating the animal uphill on his way to Old Panama to bring back a party of tourists visiting the ruins. How he expected the decrepit beast to carry four more persons was a mystery. When the harness was lifted there was disclosed the expected half–dozen large raw sores. We tied the animal in the shade near hay and water and adjourned to the station.

The coachman, a weary, unshaven Spaniard whose red eyelids showed lack of sleep, was weeping copiously. He claimed to be a madrileno—which was evident; that he had been a coachman in Spain and Panama all his life without ever before having been arrested—which was possible. He was merely one of many drivers for a livery–stable owner in Panama. Ordered to go for the tourists, he had called his employer's attention to the danger of crossing Zone territory with a horse in that condition; but the owner had ordered him to cover up the sores with pads and harness and drive along.

It was a very sad case. Here was a poor, honest coachman struggling to support a wife and I don't recall how many children, but any number sounds quite reasonable in Panama, who was about to be punished for the fault of another. The paradox of honest and coachman did not strike me until later. He was certainly telling the truth—you come to recognize it readily in all ordinary cases after a few weeks in plain clothes. The real culprit was, of course, the employer. My righteous wrath demanded that he and not his poor serf be punished. I could not release the driver. But I would see that the truth was brought out in court next morning and a warrant sworn out against the owner. With showering tears and rib–shaking sobs the coachman promised to tell the judge the whole story. I went through him, and locking him up with assurances of my deepest sympathy and full assistance, stilted on toward the little village of shacks scattered out of sight among the hills, and valleys across the border.

Coachman, witnesses, and arresting officer, to say nothing of horse, carriage, and sores were on hand when court opened next morning. As I expected, the judge failed to ask the poor fellow a single question that would bring out the complicity of his employer; did not in fact discover there was an employer. I asked to be sworn, and gave the true version of the case. The judge listened earnestly. When I had ended, he recalled the coachman. The latter expressed his astonishment that I should have made any such statements. He denied them in toto. His employer had nothing whatever to do with the case. The fault was entirely his, and no one else was in the remotest degree connected with the matter.

"Five dollars!" snapped the judge.

The coachman paid, hitched up the rat of a horse, and wabbled away into Panama.

Police business, taking me down into "the Grove" that night, I found the driver, clean–shaven and better dressed, waiting for fares before the principal house of that section.

"What kind of a game—," I began.

"Senor," he cried, and tears again seemed on the point of falling, "every word I told you was true. But of course I couldn't testify against the patron. He'd discharge me and blackmail me, and you know I have a wife and innumerable children to support. Come on over and have a drink."

This justice business, one soon learns, is of the same infallible stuff as the rest of life. After all it is only the personal opinion of the judge between two persons swearing on oath to diametrically opposed statements; and for all the impressiveness of deep furrowed brows I did not find that the average judge had any more power of reading human nature than the average of the rest of us. I well remember the morning when a meek little

Panamanian was testifying in his own behalf, in Spanish of course, when the judge broke in without even asking for a translation of the testimony:

"That'll do! Because of your gestures I believe you are trying to bunco this court. You are lying—tell him that," this to the negro interpreter; and he therewith sentenced the witness to jail.

As if any Panamanian could talk earnestly of anything without waving his arms about him.

The telephone—bell rang one afternoon. It was always doing that, twenty—four hours a day; but this time it sounded especially sharp and insistent. In the adjoining room, over the "blotter," snapped the brusk stereotyped nasal reply:

"Ancon! Bingham talking!"

The instrument buzzed a moment and the deskman looked up to say:

"'Andy' and a nigger just fell over into Pedro Miguel locks. They're sending in his body. The nigger lit on his head and hurt his leg."

His body! How uncanny it sounded! "Andy," that bunch of muscles who had made such short work of the circus wrestler in Gatun and whom I had seen not twenty—four hours before bubbling with life was now a "body." Things happen quickly on the Zone, and he whom the fates have picked to go generally shows no hesitation in his exit. But at least a man who dies for the I. C. C. has the affairs he left behind him attended to in a thorough manner. In ten minutes to a half—hour one of the Z. P. is on the ground taking note of every detail of the accident. A special train or engine rushes the body to the morgue in Ancon hospital grounds. A coroner's jury is soon meeting under the chairmanship of a policeman, long reports of everything concerning the victim or the accident are soon flowing Administration—ward. The police accident report is detailed and in triplicate. There is sure to be in the "personal files" at Culebra a history of the deceased and the names of his nearest relative or friend both on the Isthmus and in the States; for every employee must make out his biography at the time of his engagement. There are men whose regular duty it is to list and take care of his possessions down to the last lead pencil, and to forward them to the legal heirs. A year's pay goes to his family—were as

111

much required of every employer and his the burden of proving the accident the fault of the employee, how the safety appliances in factories would multiply. There is a man attached to Ancon hospital whose unenviable duty it is to write a letter of condolence to the relatives in the States.

And so the "Kangaroos" or the "Red Men" or whatever his lodge was filed behind the I. C. C. casket to the church in Ancon, and "Andy" was laid away under another of the simple white iron crosses that thickly populate many a Zone hillside, and he was charged up to the big debit column of the costs of the canal. On the cross is his new number; for officially a "Zoner" is always a number; that of the brass–check he wears as a watch–charm alive, that at the head of his grave when his canal–digging is over.

Late one unoccupied afternoon I picked up the path behind the Administration Building and, skirting a Zone residence, began to climb that famous oblong mound that dominates the Pacific end of the landscape from every direction,—Ancon Hill. For a way a fairly steep and stony path lead through thick undergrowth. Then this ceased, and a far steeper trail zigzagged up the face of the bare mountain, covered only with thin dead grass. The setting sun cast its shadow obliquely across the summit when I reached it,—a long ridge, with groves of trees, running off abruptly toward the sea. On the opposite side Uncle Sam was cutting away a whole side of the hill. But the five o'clock whistle had blown, and whole armies of little workmen swarmed across all the landscape far below, and silence soon settled down save for the dredges at Balboa that chug on through the night. But for myself the hill was wholly unpeopled. A sturdy ocean breeze swept steadily across it. The sinking sun set the jungle afire in a spot that would have startled those who do not know that it rises in the Pacific at Panama, crude, glaring colors glowed, fading to gentler and more delicate tints, then the evening shadow that had climbed the hill with me spread like a great black veil over all the world.

But the moon nearing its full followed almost on the heels of the setting sun and, casting its half–day over a scene rich in nature and history, invited the eye to swing clear round the hazy circle. Below lay Panama dully rumbling with night traffic. Silent Ancon, still better lighted, cuddled upon the lower skirts of the hill itself. Then beyond, the curving bay, half seen, half guessed, with its long promontory dying away into the hazy moonlit distance, lighted up here and there by bush fires in the jungled hills. Some way out winked the cluster of lights that marked Las Sabanas. In front, the placid Pacific, the "South Sea" of the Spaniards, spread dimly away into the void of night, its several islands seen only by the darker darkness that marked where they lay.

On the other side of the hill the rumble of cranes and night labor came up from Balboa dock. There, began the canal, which the eye could follow away into the dim hilly inland distance—and come upon a great cluster of lights that was Corozal, then another group that was Miraflores, close followed by those of Pedro Miguel; and yet further, rising to such height as to be almost indistinguishable from the lower stars the lights of the negro cabins of upper Paraiso twinkled dimly above a broad glow that was Paraiso itself. There the vista ended. For at Paraiso the canal turns to the left for its plunge through Culebra hill, and all that follows,—Empire, Cascadas, and far Gatun, was visible only in the imagination.

If only the film of time might roll back and there pass again before our eyes all that has come to pass within sight of Ancon hilltop. Across the bay there, where now are only jungle–tangled ruins, Pizarro set out with his handful of vagabonds to conquer South America; there old Buccaneer Morgan laid his bloody hand. Back in the hills there men died by scores trying to carry a ship across the Isthmus, the Spanish viceroys passed with their rich trains, there on some unknown knoll Balboa reached four hundred years ago the climax of a career that began with stowing away in a cask and ended under the headsman's ax—no end of it, down to the "Forty–niners" going hopefully out and returning filled with gold or disease, or leaving their bones here in the jungle before they really were "Forty–niners"; on down to the railroad days with men wading in swamps with survey kits, and frequently lying down to die. Then if a bit of the future, too, could for a moment be unveiled, and one might watch the first ship glide majestically and silently into the canal and away into the jungle like some amphibious monster.

It was along in those days that we were looking for a "murderous assaulter." At a Saturday night dance in a native shack back in Miraflores bush the usual riot had broken out about midnight and a revolver had come into play. As a result there was a Peruvian mulatto up in Ancon hospital who had been shot through the mouth, the bullet being somewhere in his neck. It became my frequent duty, among other Z. P.'s, to take suspects up the hill for possible identification.

One morning I strolled into the station and fell to laughing. The early train had brought in on suspicion a Spanish laborer of twenty or twenty–two; a pretty, girlish chap with huge blue eyes over which hung long black lashes like those painted on Nurnberg dolls. No one with a shadow of faith in human nature left would have believed him capable of any crime; any one at all acquainted with Spaniards must have known he could not shoot a hare, would in fact be afraid to fire off a gun.

The fear in his big blue eyes struggled with his ingenuous, girlish smile as I marched him through the long hall full of white beds and darker inmates. The Peruvian sat bolstered up in his cot, a stoical, revengeful glare on his reddish−brown swollen face. He gazed a long minute at the boy's face, across which flitted the flush of fear and embarrassment, at the big doll's eyes, then shook a raised forefinger slowly back and forth before his nose— the negative of Spanish−speaking peoples. Then he groaned, spat in a tin−can beside him, and called for paper and pencil. In the note−book I handed him he wrote in atrociously spelled Spanish:

"The man that came to the dance with this man is the man that shot me with a bullet."

The blue−eyed boy promised to point out his companion of that night. We took the 10:55 and reached Pedro Miguel during the noon hour. Down in a box−car camp between the railroad and the canal the boy called for "Jose" and there presented himself immediately a tall, studious, solemn−faced Spaniard of spare frame, about forty, dressed in overalls and working shirt. Here was even less a criminal type than the boy.

"Senor," I asked, "did you go to the dance in Miraflores last Saturday night with this youth?"

"Si, senor."

"Then I place you under arrest. We will take the one o'clock train."

He opened his mouth to protest, but closed it again without having uttered a sound. He opened it a second time, then sat suddenly down on the low edge of the box−car porch. A more genuinely astonished man I have never seen. No actor could have approached it. Still, whatever my own conviction, it was my business to bring him before his accuser. After a time he recovered sufficiently to ask permission to change his clothes, and disappeared in one of the resident box−cars. The boy was already being fed in another. Had my prisoners been of almost any one of the other seventy−one nationalities I should not have thought of letting them out of my sight. But the Zone Spaniard's respect for law is proverbial.

"Jose! Pinched Jose!" cried his American boss, when I explained that he would find himself a man short that afternoon. "You people are sure barking up the wrong tree this time. Why, Jose has been my engineer for over two years, and the steadiest man on the Zone. He writes for some Spanish paper and tells 'em the truth over there so straight that the rest of 'em down here, the anarchists and all that bunch, are aching to get him into trouble. But they'll never get anything on Jose. Have him tell you about it in Spanish if you sabe the lingo."

But Jose was a gallego, whence instead of the voluble flood of protesting words one expects from a Spaniard on such an occasion, he wrapped himself in a stoical silence. Not until we were on our way to the railroad station did I get him to talk. Then he explained in quiet, unflowery, gestureless language.

He had come to the Canal Zone chiefly to gather literary material. Not being a man of wealth, however, nor one satisfied with superficial observation, he had sought employment at his trade as stationary engineer. Besides laying in a stock for more important writing he hoped to do in the future, he was Zone correspondent of "El Liberal" of Madrid and other Spanish cities. In the social life of his fellow-countrymen on the Isthmus he had taken no part, whatever. He was too busy. He did not drink. He could not dance; he saw no sense in squandering time in such frivolities. But ever since his arrival he had been promising himself to attend one of these wild Saturday-night debauches in the edge of the jungle that he might use a description of it in some later work. So he had coaxed his one personal friend, the boy, to go with him. It was virtually the one thing besides work that he had ever done on the Zone. They had stayed two hours, and had left the moment the trouble began. Yet here he was arrested.

I bade him cheer up, to consider the trip to Ancon merely an afternoon excursion on government pass. He remained downcast.

"But think of the experience!" I cried. "Now you can tell exactly how it feels to be arrested—first-hand literary material."

But he was not philosopher enough to look at it from that point of view. To his Spanish mind arrest, even in innocence, was a disgrace for which no amount of "material" could compensate. It is a common failing. How many of us set out into the world for experience, yet growl with rage or sit downcast and silent all the way from Pedro Miguel to Panama if one such experience gives us a rough half–hour, or robs us of ten minutes sleep.

At the hospital the Peruvian gurgled and spat, beckoned for paper and wrote:

"This is the man."

"What man?" I asked.

"The man who came with that man," he scribbled, nodding his heavy face toward the blue–eyed boy.

"But is this the man that shot you?" I demanded.

"The man who came with that man is the one," he scrawled.

"Well, then this is the man that shot you?" I cried.

But he would not answer definitely to that, but sat a long time glaring out of his swollen, vindictive countenance propped up in his pillows at the tall, solemn correspondent. By and by he motioned again for paper.

"I think so. I am not sure," he miswrote.

I did NOT think so, and as the sum total of his descriptions of his assailant during the past several days amounted to "a tall man, rather short, with a face and two eyes"—he was very insistent about the eyes, which is the reason the doll–eyed boy had fallen into the drag–net—I permitted myself to accept my own opinion as evidence. The Peruvian was in all likelihood in no condition to recognize a man from a loup–garou by the time the fracas started. Much ardent water had flowed that night. I took the suspects down to Ancon station and let them cool off in porch rocking–chairs. Then I gave them passes back to Pedro Miguel for the evening train. The doll–eyed boy smiled girlishly upon me as he descended the steps, but the correspondent strode slowly away with the downcast, cheerless countenance of a man who has been hurt beyond recovery.

There were strangely contrasted days in the "gum–shoe's" calendar. Two examples taken almost at random will give the idea. On May twentieth I lolled all day in a porch rocker at Ancon station, reading a novel. Along in the afternoon Corporal Castillo drifted in. For a time he stood leaning against the desk–rail, his felt hat pushed far back on his head, his eyes fixed on some point in the interior of China. Then suddenly he snatched up a sheet of I. C. C. stationery, dropped down at a typewriter, and wrote at express speed a letter in Spanish. Next he grasped a telephone and, in the words of the deskman, "spit Spig into the 'phone" for several minutes. That over he caught up an envelope, sealed the letter and addressed it. An instant later the station was in an uproar looking for a stamp. One was found, the Corporal stuck it on the letter, fell suddenly motionless and stared for a long time at vacancy. Then a new thought struck him. He jerked open a drawer of the "gum–shoe" desk, flung the letter inside—where I found it accidentally one day some weeks afterward—and dropping into the swivel–chair laid his feet on the "gum–shoe" blotter and a moment later seemed to have fallen asleep.

By all of which signs those of us who knew him began to suspect that the Corporal had something on his mind. Not a few considered him the best detective on the force; at least he was different enough from a printer's ink detective to be a real one. But naturally the strain of heading a detective bureau for weeks was beginning to wear upon him.

"Damn it!" said the Corporal suddenly, opening his eyes, "I can't be in six places at once. You'll have to handle these cases," and he drew from a pocket and handed me three typewritten sheets, then drifted away into the dusk. I looked them over and returned to the porch rocker and the last chapters of the novel.

A meek touch on the leg awoke me at four next morning. I looked up to see dimly a black face under a khaki helmet bent over me whispering, "It de time, sah," and fade noiselessly away. It was the frontier policeman carrying out his orders of the night before. For once there was not a carriage in sight. I stumbled sleepily down into Panama and for some distance along Avenida Central before I was able to hail an all night hawk chasing a worn little wreck of a horse along the macadam. I spread my lanky form over the worn cushions and we spavined along the graveled boundary line, past the Chinese cemetery where John can preserve and burn joss to his ancestors to the end of time, out through East Balboa just awakening to life, and reached Balboa docks as day was breaking. I was not long there, and the equine caricature ambled the three miles back to town in what seemed reasonable time, considering. As we turned again into Avenida Central my watch told me there was time and to spare to catch the morning passenger. I was not a little surprised therefore to hear just then two sharp rings on the station gong. I dived headlong into the station and brought up against a locked gate, caught a glimpse of two or three ladies weeping and the tail of the passenger disappearing under the bridge. Americans have introduced the untropical idea of starting their trains on time, to the disgust of the "Spig" in general and the occasional discomfiture of Americans. I dashed wildly out through the station, across Panama's main street, down a rugged lane to the first steps descending to the track, and tumbled joyously onto a slowly moving train—to discover that it was the Balboa labor-train and that the Colon passenger was already half-way to Diablo Hill.

A Panama policeman of dusky hue, leaning against a gate-post, eyed me drowsily as I slowly climbed the steps, mopping my brow and staring at my watch.

"What time does that 6:35 train leave?" I demanded.

"Yo, senor," he said with ministerial dignity, shifting slowly to the other shoulder, "no tengo conocimiento de esas cosas" (I have no knowledge of those things).

He probably did not know there is a railroad from Panama to Colon. It has only been in operation since 1855.

Later I found the fault lay with my brass watch.

With a perspiration up for all day I set out along the track. Hounding Diablo Hill the realization that I was hungry came upon me simultaneously with the thought that unless I got through the door of Corozal hotel by 7:30 I was likely to remain so. Breakfast over, I caught the morning supply-train to Miraflores, there to dash through the locks for a five-minute interview. I walked to Pedro Miguel and, descending from the embankment of the main line, "nailed" a dirt-train returning empty and stood up for a breezy ride down through the "cut." It was the same old smoky, toilsome place, a perceptible bit lower. As in the case of a small boy only those can see its growth who have been away for a time. The train stopped with a jerk at the foot of Culebra. I walked a half-mile and caught a loaded dirt-train to Cascadas. The matter there to be investigated required ten minutes. That over, I "got in touch" at the nearest telephone, and the Corporal's voice called for my immediate presence at headquarters. There chanced to be passing through

118

Cascadas at that moment a Panama–bound freight, the caboose of which caught me up on the fly; and forty minutes later I was racing up the long stairs.

There I learned among other things that a man I was anxious to have a word with was coming in on the noon train, but would be unavailable after arrival. I sprang into a cab and was soon rolling away again, past the Chinese cemetery. At the commissary crossing in East Balboa we were held up by an empty dirt–train returning from the dump. I tossed a coin at the cabman and scrambled aboard. The train raced through Corozal, down the grade and around the curve at unslacking speed. I dropped off in front of Miraflores police station, keeping my feet, thanks to practice and good luck, and dashing up through the village, dragged myself breathlessly aboard the passenger train as its head and shoulders had already disappeared in the tunnel.

The ticket–collector pointed out my man to me in the first passenger coach, the "ladies' car"—he is a school–teacher and tobacco smoke distresses him—and by the time we pulled into Panama I had the desired information. Dinner was not to be thought of; I had barely time to dash through the second–class gate and back along the track to Balboa labor–train. From the docks a sand– train carried me to Pedro Miguel.

There was a craneman in Bas Obispo "cut" whose testimony was wanted. I reached him by two short walks and a ride. His statements suggested the advisability of questioning his room– mate, a towerman in Miraflores freight–yards. Luck would have it that my chauffeur friend——was just then passing with an I. C. C. motor–car and only a photographer for a New York weekly aboard. I found room to squeeze in. The car raced away through the "cut," up the declivity, and dropped me at the foot of the tower. The room– mate referred me to a locomotive engineer and, being a towerman, gave me the exact location of his engine. I found it at the foot of Cucaracha slide with a train nearly loaded. By the time the engineer had added his whit of information, we were swinging around toward the Pacific dump. I dropped off and, climbing up the flank of Ancon hill, descended through the hospital grounds.

Where the royal palms are finest and there opens out the broadest view of Panama, Ancon, and the bay, I gave myself five minutes' pause, after which a carriage bore me to a shop near Cathedral Plaza where second–hand goods are bought—and no questions asked. On the way back to Ancon station I visited two similar establishments.

I had been lolling in the swivel–chair a full ten minutes, perhaps, when the telephone rang. It was "the Captain" calling for me. When I reached the third–story back he handed me extradition papers to the Secretary of Foreign Affairs in Panama. A half–hour later, wholly outstripping the manana idea, I had signed a receipt for the Jap in question and transferred him from Panama to Ancon jail. Whereupon I descended to the evening passenger and rode to Pedro Miguel for five minutes' conversation, and caught the labor–train Panamaward. At Corozal I stepped off for a word with the officer on the platform and the labor–train plunged on again, after the fashion of labor–trains, spilling the last half of its disembarking passengers along the way. Ten minutes later the headlight of the last passenger swung around the curve and carried me away to Panama.

That might have done for the day, but I had gathered a momentum it was hard to check. Not long after returning from the police mess to the swivel chair a slight omission in the day's program occurred to me. I called up Corozal police station.

"What?" said a mashed–potato voice at the other end of the wire.

"Who's talking?"

"Policeman Green, sah."

"Station commander there?"

"No, sah. Station commander he gone just over to de Y. M. to play billiards, sah. Dey one big match on to–night."

Of course I could have "got" him there. But on second thoughts it would be better to see him in person and clear up at the same time a little matter in one of the labor camps, and not run the risk of causing the loss of the billiard championship. Besides Corozal is cooler to sleep in than Ancon. In a black starry night I set out along the invisible railroad for the first station.

An hour later, everything settled to my satisfaction, I had discovered a vacant bed in Corozal bachelor quarters and was pulling off my coat preparatory to the shower–bath and a well– earned night's repose. Suddenly I heard a peculiar noise in the adjoining room, much like that of a seal coming to the surface after being long under water. My curiosity awakened, I sauntered a few feet along the veranda. Beside one of the cots stood a short, roly–poly little man, the lower third of whom showed rosy pink below his bell–shaped white nightie. As he turned his face toward the light to switch it off I swallowed the roof of my mouth and clawed at the clap–boarding for support. It was "the Sloth!" He had been transferred. I slipped hastily into my coat and, turning up the collar, plunged out into the rain and the night and stumbled blindly away on weary legs towards Panama.

CHAPTER IX

There were four of us that Sunday. "Bish" and I always went for an afternoon swim unless police or mess duties forbade. Then there was Bridgley, who had also once displayed his svelte form in a Z. P. uniform to admiring tourists, but was now a pursuer of "soldiering" Hindus on Naos Island. I wish I could describe Bridgley for you. But if you never knew him ten pages would give you no clearer idea, and if you ever did, the mere mention of the name Bridgley will be full and ample description. Still, if you must have some sort of a lay figure to hang your imaginings on, think of a man who always reminds you of a slender, delicate porcelain vase of great antiquity that you know a strong wind would smash to fragments,—yet when you accidentally swat it off the mantelpiece to the floor it bobs up without a crack. Then you grow bolder and more curious and jump on it with both feet in your hob–nailed boots, and to your astonishment it not only does not break but—

Well, Bridgley was one of us that Sunday afternoon; and then there was "the Admiral," well–dressed as always, who turned up at the last moment; for which we were glad, as any one would be to have "the Admiral" along. So we descended into Panama by the train– guard short–cut and across the bridge that humps its back over the P. R. R. like a cat in unsocial mood, and on through Caledonia out along the beach sands past the old iron hulls about which Panamanian laborers are always tinkering under the impression that they are working. This time we walked. I don't recall now whether it was quarter–cracks, or the Lieutenant hadn't slept well—no, it couldn't have been that, for the Lieutenant never let his personal mishaps trample on his good nature—or whether "Bish" had decided to try to reduce weight. At any rate we were afoot, and thereby hangs the tale—or as much of a tale as there is to tell.

We tramped resolutely on along the hard curving beach past the disheveled bath–houses before which ladies from the Zone gather in some force of a Sunday afternoon. For this time we were really out for a swim rather than to display our figures. On past the light–brown bathers, and the chocolate–colored bathers, and the jet black bathers who seemed to consider that color covering enough, till we came to the big silent saw–mill at the edge of the cocoanut grove that we had been invited long since to make a Z. P. dressing–room.

Before us spread the reposing, powerful, sun–shimmering Pacific. Across the bay, clear as an etching, lay Panama backed by Ancon hill. In regular cadence the ocean swept in with a hoarse, resistless roll on the sands.

We dived in, keeping an eye out for the sharks we knew never come so far in and probably wouldn't bite if they did. The sun blazed down white hot from a cloudless sky. This time the Lieutenant and Sergeant Jack had not been able to come, but we arranged the races and jumps on the sand for all that, and went into them with a will and—

A rain–drop fell. Nor was it long lonesome. Before we had finished the hundred–yard dash we were in the midst of——it was undeniably raining. Half a moment later "bucketsful" would have been a weak simile. All the pent up four months of an extra long rainy season seemed to have been loosed without warning. The blanket of water blotted out Panama and Ancon hill across the bay, blotted out the distant American bathers, then the light–brown ones, then the chocolate–tinted, then even the jet black ones close at hand.

We remained under water for a time to keep dry. But the rain whipped our faces as with thousands of stinging lashes. We crawled out and dashed blindly up the bank toward the saw–mill, the rain beating on our all but bare skins, feeling as it might to stand naked in Miraflores locks and let the sand pour down upon us from sixty feet above. When at last we stumbled under cover and up the stairs to where our clothing hung, it was as if a weight of many tons had been lifted from our shoulders.

The saw–mill was without side–walls; consisted only of a sheet– iron roof and floors, on the former of which the storm pounded with a roar that made only the sign language feasible. It was now as if we were surrounded on all sides by solid walls of water and forever shut off from the outer world—if indeed that had survived. Sheets of water slashed in further and further across the floor. We took to huddling behind beams and under saw–benches —the militant storm hunted us out and wetted us bit by bit. "The Admiral" and I tucked ourselves away on the 45–degree eye–beams up under the roaring roof. The angry water gathered together in columns and swept in and up to soak us.

At the end of an hour the downpour had increased some hundred per cent. It was as if an express train going at full speed had gradually doubled its rapidity. That was the day when little harmless streams tore themselves apart into great gorges and left their pathetic little bridges alone and deserted out in the middle of the gulf. That was the famous May twelfth, 1912, when Ancon recorded the greatest rainfall in her history,—7.23 inches, virtually all within three hours. Three of us were ready to surrender and swim home through it. But there was "the Admiral" to consider. He was dressed clear to his scarf–pin—and Panama tailors tear horrible holes in a police salary. So we waited and dodged and squirmed into closer holes for another hour; and grew steadily wetter.

Then at length dusk began to fall, and instead of slacking with the day the fury of the storm increased. It was then that "the Admiral" capitulated, seeing fate plainly in league with his tailor; and wigwagging the decision to us beside him, he led the way down the stairs and dived into the world awash.

Wet? We had not taken the third step before we were streaming like fire hose. There was nearly an hour of it, splashing knee–deep through what had been when we came out little dry sandy hollows; steering by guess, for the eye could make out nothing fifty yards ahead, even before the cheese–thick darkness fell; bowed like nonogenarians under the burden of water; staggering back and forth as the storm caught us crosswise or the earth gave way under us. "The Admiral's" patent–leather shoes—but why go into painful details? Those who were in Panama on that memorable afternoon can picture it all for themselves, and the others will never know. The wall of water was as thick as ever when we fought our bowed and weary way up over the railroad bridge and, summoning up the last strength, splurged tottering into "Angelini's."

When our streaming had so far subsided that they recognised us for solvent human beings, encouraging concoctions were set before us. Bridgley, fearing the after effects, acquired a further quart bottle of protection, and when we had gathered force for the last dash we plunged out once more toward our several goals. As the door of 111 slammed behind me, the downpour suddenly slackened. As I paused before my room to drain, it stopped raining.

123

I supped on bread, beer, and cheese from over the frontier—we had arrived thirty seconds too late for Ancon police mess. Then when I had saved what was salvable from the wreckage and reclad in such wardrobe as had luckily remained at home, I strolled over toward the police station to put in a serene and quiet evening.

But it has long since been established that troubles flock together. As I crunched up the gravel walk between the hedge–rows, wild riot broke on my ear. Ancon police station was in eruption. From the Lieutenant to the newest uniformless "rookie" every member of the force was swarming in and out of the building. The Zone and Panama telephones were ringing in their two opposing dialects, the deskman was shouting his own peculiar brand of Spanish into one receiver and bawling English at the other, all hands were diving into old clothes, the most apathetic of the force were girding up their loins with the adventurous fire of the old Moro–hunting days in their eyes, and all, some ahorse, more afoot, were dashing one by one out into the night and the jungle.

It was several minutes before I could catch the news. At last it was shouted at me over a telephone. Murder! A white Greek—who ever heard of a colored Greek?—with a white shirt on had shot a man at Pedro Miguel at 6:35. Every road and bypath of escape to Panama was already blocked, armed men would meet the assassin whatever way he might take. I went down to meet the evening train, resolved after that to strike out into the night in the random hope of having my share in the chase. It had begun to rain again, but only moderately, as if it realized it could never again equal the afternoon record.

Then suddenly the excitement exploded. It was only a near–murder. Two Colombians had been shot, but would in all probability recover. The news reached me as I stood at the second–class gate scanning the faces of the great multicolored river of passengers that poured out into the city. For two hours, one by one with crestfallen mien, the manhunters leaked back into Ancon station and, the case having dwindled to one of regular daily routine, by eleven we were all abed.

In the morning the "Greek chase" fell to me. More detailed description of the culprit had come in during the night, including the bit of information that he was a bad man from the Isle of Crete. The belt–straining No. 38 oiled and loaded, I set off on an assignment that was at least a relief after pursuing stolen necklaces for negro women, or crowbars lost by the I. C. C.

124

Zone Policeman 88

By nine I was climbing to Pedro Miguel police station on its knoll with the young Greek who had exchanged hats with the assassin after the crime. That afternoon a volunteer joined me. He was a friend of the wounded men, a Peruvian black as jade, but without a suggestion of the negro in anything but his outward appearance. He was of the size and build of a Sampson in his prime, spoke a Spanish so clear—cut it seemed to belie his African blood, and had the restless vigor acquired in a youth of tramping over the Andine ranges.

I piled him into a cab and we rolled away to East Balboa, to climb upon an empty dirt—train and drop off as it raced through Miraflores, the sturdy legs of the Peruvian saving him where his practice would not have. Up in the bush between Pedro Miguel and Paraiso we found a hut where the Greek had stopped for water and gone on up a gully. We set out to follow, mounting partly on hands and knees, partly dragging ourselves by grass and bushes up what had been and would soon be again a torrential mountain stream. For hours we tore through the jungle, up hills steeper than the path of righteousness, following now a few faint foot—prints or trampled bushes, now a hint from some native bush dweller. The rain outside vied with the sweat within as to which would first soak us through. To make things merrier I had not only to wear an arsenal but a coat atop to conceal it from the general public.

To mention the holes I crawled into and the clues I followed during the next few days would be more tiresome than a Puritan prayer. By day I was dashing back and forth through all Ancon district, by night prowling about the grimier sections of Panama city. Almost daily I got near enough to sniff the prey. Now it was a Greek confectioner on Avenida Central who admitted that the fugitive had called on him during the night, now a Panamanian pesquisa whose stool—pigeon had seen him out in the bush, then the information that he had stopped to shave and otherwise alter his appearance in some shack half—way across the Zone and afterward struck off for Panama by an unused route. The clues were pendulum— like. They took me a half—dozen times at least out the winding highway to Corozal, on to Miraflores and even further. The rainy season and the reign of umbrellas had come. It had been formally opened on that memorable Sunday afternoon. There was still sunshine at times, but always a wet season heaviness to the atmosphere; and the rains were already giving the rolling jungle hills a tinge of new green. There was nothing to be gained by hurrying. The fugitive was as likely to crawl forth from one place as another along the rambling road. Here I paused to kill a lizard or to watch the clumsy march of one of the huge purple and many— colored land-crabs, there to gaze away across a jungled valley soft and fuzzy in the humid air like some Corot painting.

I even sailed for San Francisco in the quest. For of course each outgoing ship must be searched. One day I had word that a "windjammer" was about to sail; and racing out to Balboa I was soon set aboard the fore and aft schooner Meteor far out in the bay. When I plunged down into the cabin the peeled–headed German captain was seated at a table before a heap of "Spig" dollars, paying off his black shore hands. He solemnly asserted he had no Greek aboard, and still more solemnly swore that if he found one stowed away he would turn him over to the police in San Francisco —which was kind of him but would not have helped matters. There are several men running gaily about San Francisco streets who would be very welcome in certain quarters on the Zone and sure of lodging and food for a long time to come.

By this time the tug Bolivar had us in tow, the captain went racing over his ship like any of his crew, tugging at the ropes, and we were gliding out across Panama bay, past the little greening islands, the curving panorama of the city and Ancon hill growing smaller and smaller behind—bound for 'Frisco. What ho! the merry "windjammer" with her stowed sails and smell of tar awakened within me old memories, hungry and grimy for the most part. But this was no independent, self–respecting member of the Wind–wafted sisterhood. Far out in the offing lay a steamer of the same line that was to TOW the Meteor to the Golden Gate! How is the breed of sailors fallen! The few laborers aboard would take an occasional wheel, pick oakum, and yarn their unadventurous yarns. As we drew near, a boat was lowered to set me aboard the steamer, to the rail–crowding surprise of her passengers, who fancied they had hours since seen the last of Zone and "Zoners." The captain asserted he had nothing aboard grown nearer Greece than three Irishmen, any one of whom—facetiousness seemed to be one of the captain's characteristics—I might have and welcome. A few moments later I was back aboard the tug waving farewell to steamer and "windjammer" as they pushed away into the twilight sea, and the Bolivar turned shoreward.

I received a "straight tip" one evening that the fugitive Greek was hiding in a hovel on the Cruces trail. What part of the Cruces trail, the informant did not hint; but he described the hut in some detail. So next morning as the thick gray dawn of this tropical land was melting into day, I descended at Bas Obispo, through the canal to Gamboa and struck off into the dense dripping jungle. The rainy season had greened things up and gone—

temporarily, of course, for in a day or two it would be on us again in all tropical fury. In the few days since the first rain the landscape had changed like a theater decoration, a green not even to be imagined in the temperate zone.

It turned out that the ancient village of Cruces was a mere two- mile stroll from the canal, a thatch-roofed native town of some thirty dwellings on the rocky shore of an inner curve of the Chagres, where travelers from Balboa to the last "Forty-niner" disembarked from their thirty-six mile ride up the river and struck on along the ten-mile road through the jungle to Panama— the famous Cruces trail. Except for its associations the village was without interest—except some personal Greek interest. Sour looks were chiefly my portion, for the villagers have never taken kindly to Americans.

I soon sought out the trail, here a mere path undulating through rank, wet-hot, locust singing jungle. Here in the tangled somber mystery of the wilderness grew every tropical thing; countless giant ferns, draping tangles of vines, the mango tree with its rounded dome of leaves like the mosque of Omar done in greenery, the humble pineapple with its unproportionate fruit, everywhere the banana, king of vegetables, clothed in its own immense leaves, the frondy zapote, now and then in a hollow a clump of yellowish-green bamboo, though not numerous or nearly so large as in many another tropical land, above all else the symmetrical Gothic fronds of the palm nodding in a breeze the more humble vegetation could not know. The constant music of insect life sounded in my ears; everywhere were flowers of brilliant hue, masses of bush blossoms not unlike the lilac in appearance, but like all down on the Isthmus, odorless—or rather with a pungent scent, like strong catsup.

Four months earlier I should have been chary of diving back into the Panamanian "bush" alone, above all on a criminal hunt. But it needs only a little time on the Zone to make one laugh at the absurd stories of danger from the bush native that are even yet appearing in many U. S. papers. They are not over friendly to whites, it is true. But they were all of that familiar languid Central American type, blinking at me apathetically out of the shade of their huts, crowding to one edge of the trail as I passed, eying me silently, a bit morosely, somewhat frightened because their experience of Americans is of a discourteous creature who shouts at them in a strange tongue and swears at them because they do not understand it. The moment they heard their own customary greetings they changed to children delighted to do anything to oblige—even to the extent of dragging their indolent forms erect to lead the way a quarter-mile through the bush to some isolated shack. Far from contemplating any injury, all these wayward children of the jungle ask is to be let alone to drift through life in their own way. Still more absurd is the notion of danger from wild beasts—other than the tiny wild beast that burrows its painful way under the skin.

So I pushed on, halting at many huts to make covert inquiries. It was a joyous, brilliant day overhead. Down in the dense, rampant, singing jungle I sweated profusely—and enjoyed it. Choking for a drink in a hutless section, I took one of the crooked, tunnel–like trails to the left in the direction of the Chagres. But it squirmed off through thick jungle, through banana groves and untended pineapple gardens to come out at last at an astonished hut on a knoll, from which was not to be seen a sign of the river. I crawled through another struggling side–trail further on and this time reached the stream, but at a bank too sheer and bush– matted to descend. The third attempt brought me to where the river made a graceful bend at my feet and I descended an abrupt jungle bank to drink and stroll a bit along the stony shore; then plunged in for a swim. It was just the right temperature, with dense jungle banks on either side like great green unscalable walls, the water clear and a bit over waist deep in the middle of the stream. Now and then around the one or the other bend came a cayuca, the native dug–out made of the hollowed trunk of a tree, usually the cedro—though to a jungle native any tree is a "cedro" if he does not happen to think of its right name. Twenty to thirty feet long, sometimes piled high with vegetables, sometimes with several natives seated Indian file in the bottom, the gunwales a bare two or three inches above the water, they needed nice management, especially in the rapids below Cruces. The locomotive power, generally naked to the waist, stood up in the craft and climbed his polanca, or long pike pole, hand over hand, every naked brown muscle in play, moving in perfect rhythm and apparent ease even up–stream against the powerful current.

Soon after Chagres and trail parted company, the former to wind on up through the jungle hills to its birthplace in the land of Darien and wild Indians, the latter to strike for the Pacific. Over a mildly rough country it led, down into tangled ravines, up over dense forested hillocks where the jungle had been fought back by Uncle Sam and on the brows of which I halted to drink of the fresh breeze sweeping across from the Atlantic. All this time not a suggestion of anything Greek, though I managed by some simple strategy to cast a sweeping glance into every hovel along the way.

Then came the real Cruces trail—the rest only follows the general direction. I fell upon it unexpectedly. It is still there as it was when the Peruvian viceroys and their glittering trains clattered along it, surprisingly well preserved; a cobbled way some three feet wide of that rough and bumpy variety the Spaniard even to–day fancies a real road, broken in places but still well marked, leading away southward through the wilderness.

Overhead were tall spreading trees laden with blossomless orchids. Under some of them was broad grassy shade; but the surrounding wall of vegetation cut off all breeze. The way was intersected by many roads of leaf–cutting ants, as level, wide and well–built in their proportion as the old Roman highways, with such an industrious throng going and coming upon them as one could find nowhere equaled, unless it be on the Grand Trunk Road of India.

Then suddenly there appeared the hut that had been described to me. I surrounded it and, hand upon the butt of my No. 38, closed in upon the place, then rushed it with all forces.

There was not a sign of human life in the vicinity. The door was tied shut with a single strand of old rope, but there was no question that the fugitive might be hiding inside, for the reed walls had holes in them large enough to drive a sheep through, and there was nothing within to hide behind. I thrust an arm through an opening and dragged the large and heavy earthenware water–jar to me for a drink, and pushed on.

Squatter's cabins were now appearing, as contrasted with the native bushman's peaked hut; sleeping–places thrown together of tin cans, boxes and jungle rubbish, many negro shanties built of I. C. C. scraps—all of which announced the vicinity of the canal. Any hut might be a hiding–place. I made ostensibly casual inquiries, interlarded between stories, at several of them, and at length established that the Greek had been there not long before, but was elsewhere now. Then about four of the afternoon I burst out suddenly in sight of a broad modern highway, and leaving the ancient route as it headed away toward Old Panama, I turned aside to the modern city.

Then I was "called off the Greek chase"; and a couple of evenings later, along with the evening train and the evening fog, the Inspector "blew in" from his forty–two days' vacation in the States, like a breath from far–off Broadway. Buffalo Bill had been duly opened and started on his season's way, the absent returned, and Corporal Castillo suddenly dwindled again to a mere corporal.

As everything must have its flaws, perhaps the chief one that might be charged against the Z. P. is "red tape." Strictly speaking it is no Z. P. fault at all, but a weakness of all government. One example will suffice.

During the month of May I was assigned the investigation of certain alleged conditions in Panama's restricted district. The then head of the plain–clothes division gave me carte blanche, but suggested that I need not spare my expense account in libating the various establishments until I "got acquainted" sufficiently with the inmates to pick up indirectly the information desired.

Which general line I followed and, the information having been gathered and the report made up, I proceed to make out my expenditures of $45 for the month to forward to Empire for reimbursement. Now it needs no deep detective experience to know that in such cases you naturally begin with, "Well, what you going to drink, girls?" and end by paying the bill in a lump sum—a large lump sum—and go your way in peace. What more then could I do than set down such items as:

"May 12, Liquor, investigation, Panama—$6.50?"

But here I began to feel the tangling strands. Was it not stated that all applications for reimbursement required an exact itemized account of each separate expenditure, with the price of each? It did. But in the first place I did not know half the beverages consumed in that investigation by sight, smell, or name. In the second place I came ostensibly as a "rounder"; it would perhaps have been advisable at the close of each evening's entertainment to draw out note–book and pencil and starting the round of the table announce:

"Now, girls, I'm a dee–tective. No, keep yer places, I ain't going to pinch nobody. Anyhow I'm only a Zone detective. But I just want to ask you a few questions. Now, Mamie, what's that you're drinking? Ah! A gin ricky. And just how much does that cost—here? And you, Flossie? An absinthe frappe? Ah! Very good. And what is the retail price of that particular drink?"—and so on ad nauseum.

"Very true," replied authority, "that would of course be impossible. But to be reimbursed you must set down in detail every item of expenditure, and its price."

Reason and government red tape move in two parallel lines, with the usual meeting–place.

Nor was that all. While the black Peruvian was on my staff I gave him money for food. It was not merely expected, it was definitely so ordered. Yet when I set down:

"May 27, To Peruvian for food—$.50." authority threw up its hands in horror. Did I not know that reimbursements were ONLY for "liquor and cigars, cab or boat hire, and meals away from home?" I did. But I also knew that superiors had ordered me to feed the Peruvian. "To be sure!" cried astounded authority. "But you set down such an expenditure as follows:

"'May 27, Two bottles of beer, Pan., investigation—$.50.'

"And as you are allowed cab fare ONLY for yourself, when you take the Peruvian or any one else out to Balboa in a cab you set down the item:

"'May 26, Cab, Ancon to Balboa AND RETURN, investigation—$1.'"

The upshot of all which was, not feeling able with all my patriotism to "set up" $45 worth of mixed drinks for Uncle Sam, I was forced to open another investigation and gather from all the Z. P. authorities on the subject, from Naos Island to Paraiso, the name and price of every known beverage. Then when I had fitted together a picture puzzle of these that summed up to the amount I had actually spent, I was called upon to sign a statement thereunder that "this is a true and exact account of expenditures during the month of May. So help me God."

But then, as I have said before, these things are not Z. P. faults, they are the faults of government since government began.

It had become evident soon after the Inspector's return that unless crime began to pick up down at the Pacific end of the Zone, I should find myself again banished to the foreign land of Gatun. For there had been a distinct rise in the criminal commodity at that end during the past weeks. The premonition soon fell true.

"Take the 10:55 to Gatun," said the Inspector one morning, without looking up from his filing case, "Corporal Macey will tell you about it when you get there,"

CHAPTER X

"Why, the fact is," said Corporal Macey, lighting his meerschaum pipe until the match burned down to his fingers," several little burglary stunts have been pulling themselves off since the sergeant went on vacation. But the most aggrayvaatin' is this new one of twenty–two quarts of good Canadian Club bein' maliciously extracted from St. Martin's saloon last night."

From which important beginning I fell quickly back into the old life again, derelicting about Gatun and vicinity by day, wandering the nights away in black, noisy New Gatun and along the winding back road under the cloud–scudding sky. Yet it was a different life. Gatun had changed. Even her concrete light–house was winking all night now up among the I. C. C. dwellings. The breeze from off the Caribbean was heavy and lifeless. The landscape looked wet and lush and rampant, of a deep–seated green, and instead of the china–blue skies the dull, leaden–gray heavens seemed to hang low and heavy overhead, like a portending fate. On the winding back road the jungle trees still stood out against the night sky, at times, too, there was a moon, but only a pale silver one that peered weakly here and there through the scudding gray clouds. The air grew more thick and sultry day by day, the heat was sticky, the weather dripping, with the sun only an irregular whitish blotch in the sky. Through the open windows the heavy, damp night came miasmically floating in, the very cigarettes mildewed in my pockets. Earth and air seemed heavy and toil–bowed by comparison with other days. The jungle still hummed busily, yet, it seemed, a bit mournfully as if preparing for production and unhilarious with the task before it, like a woman first learning of her pregnancy. Life seemed to hang more heavily even on humanity; "Zoners" looked less gay and carefree than in the sunny dry season, though still far more so than in the north. One could not shake off a premonition of impending disaster in I know not what form—like that of Teufelsdroeck before he entered the "Center of Indifference."

Dr. O——– of the Sanitary Department had gone up into the interior along the Trinidad river to hunt mosquitoes. Why he went so far away for them in this season was hard to understand. There he was, however, and the order had come to bring him back to civilization. The execution thereof fell, of course, to my friend B——, who to the world at large is merely Policeman No.——, to the force "Admiral of the Inland Fleet," and in the general scheme of things is a luckier man than Vanderchild to have for his task in life the patrolling of Gatun Lake. B—— invited me to go along. There was nothing particular doing in the criminal line around Gatun just then; moreover the doctor was known to be well armed and there was no telling just how much resistance he might offer a single policeman. I accepted.

I was at the appointed rendezvous promptly at seven, a pocket filled with commissary cigars. Strict truthfulness demands the admission that it was really eight, however, when B—— came wandering down the muddy steps behind the railroad station, followed by a black prisoner with a ten–gallon can of gasoline on his head. When that had been poured into the tank, we were off across the ever–rising waters of Gatun Lake. For Gatun police launch is one of those peculiar motor–boats that starts the same day you had planned to.

It was such a day as could not have been bettered had it been made to order, with a week to think out the details,—a dry–season day even to the Atlantic breeze that goes with it, a sort of Indian summer of the rainy season; though the heavy battalions of gray clouds that hung all around the horizon as if awaiting the order to charge warned the Zone to make merry while it might, for to- morrow it would surely rain—in deluges. The lake, much higher now than in my former Gatun days, was licking at the 27–foot level that morning. Under the brilliant blue sky it looked like some vast unruffled mirror—which is no figure of speech, but plain fact.

"Through a Forest in a Motor–boat" we might have dubbed the trip. We had soon crossed the unbroken expanse of the lake and were moving through a submerged forest. Splendid royal palms stood up to their necks in the water, corpulent, century–old giants of the jungle stood on tip–toe with their jagged noses just above the surface, gasping their last. Great mango–trees laden with fruit were descending into the flood. The lake was so mirror–like we could see the heads of drowning palm–trees and the blue sky with its wisps of snow–white feathery clouds as plainly below as above, so mirror–like the protruding stump of a palm looked like a piece of just double that length and exactly equal ends floating upright like a water thermometer, so reflective that the broken end of a branch showing above the surface appeared to be an acute angle of wood floating exactly at the angle in impossible equilibrium.

Our prisoner and crew were from "Bahbaydos"—only you can't pronounce it as he did, nor make the "a" broad enough, nor show the inside of your red throat clear back to the soft palate to contrast with the glistening black skin of your carefree, grinning face. Theoretically he was being punished for assault and battery. But if this is punishment to be sentenced to cruise around on Gatun Lake I wonder crime on the Zone is so rare and unusual. This much I am sure, if I were in that particular "Badgyan's" shoes— no, he had none; but his tracks, say—the day my time ran out I should pick a quarrel with a Jamaican and leave his countenance in such a condition that the judge could find no grounds for a reasonable doubt in the matter.

We were mounting the river Trinidad. River, yes, but we followed it only because it had kept back the jungle and left a way free of tree–tops, not because there was not water enough anywhere, in any direction, to float a boat of many times our draught. Turns so sharp we rocked in our own wake; once we passed acres upon acres of big, cod–like fish floating dead upon the water among the branches and the forest rubbish. It seems the lake in rising spread over some poisonous mineral in the soil. But life there was none, except the rampant green dying plant life in every direction to the horizon. There were not even birds, other than now and then a stray snow–white slender one of the heron species that fled majestically away across the face of the nurtureless waters as we steamed—no, gasolined down upon it. Soon after leaving Gatun we had passed a couple of jungle families on their way to market in their cayucas laden with mounds of produce,—plump mangoes with a maidenly blush on either cheek, fat yellow bananas, grass–green plantains, a duck or a chicken standing tied by one leg on top of it all and gazing complacently around at the scene with the air of an experienced tourist. It was two hours later that we sighted the next human being. He was a solitary old native paddling about at the entrance to the "grass–bird region" in a huge dugout as time– scarred as himself.

It was near here that weeks before I had turned with "Admiral" B— —up a little stream now forever gone to a knoll on which sat the thatched shelter of a negro who had "taken to the bush" and refused to move even when notified that he was living on U. S. public domain. When we had knocked from the trees a box of mangoes and turkey–red maranones, B—— touched a match to the thatch roof and almost before we could regain the launch the shack was pouring skyward in a column of smoke. Even the squatter's old table and chair and a barrel of tumbled odds and ends entirely outside the hut—it had no walls—caught fire, and when, we lost sight of the knoll only the blazing stumps of the four poles that had supported the roof remained.

B—— had burned whole villages in this lake territory, after the owners with legal claims had been paid condemnation damages. Long ago the natives had been warned to move, and the banks of the lake–to–be specified. But many of these skeptical children of nature had taken this as a vain "yanqui" boast and either refused to move until burned out or had rebuilt their hovels on land that in a few months more would also be flooded.

The rescue expedition proceeded. Once we got caught in the top– most branches of a tree, released from which we pushed on along the sinuous river that had no banks. It was not hot, even at noonday. We sweated a bit in poling a thirty–foot boat out of a tree–top, but cooled again directly we were off. My kodak was far away at the other end of the Zone. But then, on second thought it was better for once to enjoy nature as it was without trying to carry it away. Kodaking is a species of covetousness, anyway, an attempt to bear away home with us and hoard for our own the best we come upon in our travels. Whereas here, of course, it was impossible. The greatest of artists could not have carried away a tenth of that scene, a scene so fascinating that though we had tossed into the bottom of the boat at the start a bundle of fresh New York papers—and fresh New York papers are not often scorned down on the Zone—they still lay in the bottom of the boat when the trip ended.

At length little thatched cottages began to appear on knolls along the way, and as we chugged our way around the tree–tops upon them the inhabitants slipped quickly into some clothes that were evidently kept for just such emergencies. Then we began nearing higher land, so that the upper and then the lower branches of the forest stood out of water, then only the ends of the lower limbs dipped in the rising flood, downcast, as if they knew the sentence of death was upon them also. For though there was sunk already beneath the flood a forest greater than ten Fontainebleaus, the lake was steadily rising a full two inches a day. Where it touched that morning the 27–foot level, in a few months more, says "the Colonel," it will reach the 87–foot level and spread over one hundred and sixty–four square miles of territory—and when "the Colonel" makes an assertion wise men hesitate to put their money on the other horse. Then will all this vast area with more green than in all the state of Missouri disappear forever beneath the flood and man may dive down, down into the forest and see what the world was like in Noah's time, and fancy the sunken cities of Holland, for many a famous route, and villages older than the days of Pizarro will be forever wiped out by the rising waters—a scene to be beheld today nowhere else, and in a few years not even here. At last we were really in a river, an overflowed river, to be sure, where it would have been hard to find a landing–place or a bank among those tree trunks knee–deep in water. We had long since crossed the Zone line, but our badges were still valid. For it has pleased the Republic of Panama, at a whispered word from "Tio Sam," to cede to the Z. P. command over all Gatun Lake and for three miles around it, as far as ever it may spread.

Then all at once we were startled by a hearty hail from among the trees and I looked up to see Y——, of the Smithsonian, fully dressed, standing waist–deep in the water at the edge of the forest, waving an insect trap in one hand.

"What the devil are you doing there?" I gasped.

"Doing? I'm taking a walk along the old Gatun–Chorrera trail, and I fancy I 'll be about the last man to travel it. Come on up to camp."

On a mango–shaped knoll thirty miles from Gatun that will also soon be lake bottom, we found a native shack transformed into the headquarters of a scientific expedition. We sat down to a frontier lunch which called for none of the excuses made for it by Y—— when he appeared in his dripping full–dress and joined us without even bothering to change his water–spurting shoes. In his boxes he had carefully stuck away side by side an untold number of members of the mosquito family. Queer vocation; but then, any vocation is good that gives an excuse to live out in this wild tropical world.

By one we had Dr. O—— aboard and were waving farewell to the camp. The return, of course, was not the equal of the outward trip; even nature cannot duplicate so perfect a thing. But two raging showers gave us views of the drowning jungle under another aspect, and between them we awakened vast rolling echoes across the silent flooded world by shooting at flocks of little birds with an army rifle that would have killed an elephant.

It is not hard to realize why the bush native does not love the American. Put yourself in his breechclout. Suppose a throng of unsympathetic foreigners suddenly appeared resolved to turn all the world you knew into a lake, just because that absurd outside world wanted to float steamers you never knew the use of, from somewhere you never heard of, to somewhere you did not know. Suppose a representative of that unsympathetic government came snorting down upon you one day in a wild fearful invention they called a motor–boat, as you were lolling under the thatch roof your grandfather built, and cried:

"Come on! Get out of here! We're going to burn your house and turn this country into a lake."

Flood the land which was your great–grand–father's, the spot where you used to play leap–frog under the banana trees, the jungle lane where your mother's courtship days were passed and the ceiga tree under which she was wedded—if matters were ever carried to that ceremonious length. What though this foreign nation gave you a bag of peculiar pieces of metal for your trouble, when you had never seen a score of such coins in your life and barely knew the use of them, being acquainted with life only as it is picked from a mango–tree? The foreigners had cried, "Take this money and go buy a farm somewhere else," and you looked around you and saw all the world you had ever really known the existence of sinking beneath the rising waters. Where would you go, think you, to buy that new farm? Even if you fled and found another unknown land high and dry, or a town, what could you do, having not the remotest idea how to live in a town with only pieces of metal to get food out of instead of the mango–tree that had stood behind the house your grandfather built ever since you were born and dropped mangoes whenever you were hungry? To say the least you would be some peeved.

It was midafternoon when the white bulk of Gatun locks rose on the horizon. Then the lake opened out, the great dam, that is rather a connecting link between two ranges of hills, spread across all the landscape, and at four I raced up the muddy steps behind the station to a telephone. Five minutes later I was hurrying away across locks and dam to the marshland beyond the Spillway to inquire who, and wherefore, had attempted to burn up the I. C. C. launch attached to dredge No.———.

My Canal Zone days were drawing rapidly to a close. I could have remained longer without regret, but the world is wide and life is short. Soon came the day, June seventeenth, when I must go back across the Isthmus to clear up the last threads of my existence as a "Zoner." Chiefly for old times' sake I dropped off at Empire. But it was not the same Empire of the census. Almost all the old crowd was gone; one by one they had "kissed the Zone good–by." "The boss" of those days had never returned, "smiling Johnny" had been transferred, even Ben had "done quit an' gone back to Bahbaydos." The Zone is like a small section of life; as in other places where generations are short one catches there a hint of what old age will be. It was like wandering over the old campus when those who were freshmen in our day had hawked their gowns and mortarboards and gone their way; I felt like a man in his dotage with only the new, unknown, and indifferent generation about him.

I went down to the old suspension bridge. Far down below was the same struggling energy, the same gangs of upright human ants, the "cut" with its jangle and jar of steam–shovels and trains still stretching away endless in either direction. Here as in the world at large generations of us may come and pass away, but the tearing of the shovels at the rocky earth, the racing of dirt–laden trains for the Pacific goes unbrokenly on, as the world and its work will continue without a pause when we are gone indeed.

Soon the water will be turned in and nine–tenths of all this labor will be submerged and forever hidden from view. The swift growth of the tropics will quickly heal the scars of the steam–shovels, and palm–trees will wave the steamer on its way through what will seem almost a natural channel. Then blase travelers lolling in their deck chairs will gaze about them and snort:

"Huh! Is that all we got for nine years' work and half a billion dollars?" They will have forgotten the scrubbing of Panama and Colon, forgotten the vast hospitals with great surgeons and graduate nurses, the building of hundreds of houses and the furnishing of them down to the last center table, they will not recall the rebuilding of the entire P. R. R., nor scores of little items like $43,000 a year merely for oil and negroes to pump it on the pestilent mosquito, the thousand and one little things so essential to the success of the enterprise yet that leave not a trace behind. Greater perhaps than the building of the canal is the accomplishment of the United States in showing the natives how life can be lived safely and healthily in tropical jungles. Yet the lesson will not be learned, and on the heels of the last canal builder will return all the old slovenliness and disease, and the native will sink back into just what he would have been had we never come.

I caught a dirt–train to Balboa. There the very town at which I had landed on the Zone five months before was being razed to give place to the permanent, reenforced–concrete city that is to be the canal headquarters. Balboa police station was only a pile of lumber, with a band of negroes drilling away the very rock on which it had stood. I took a last view of the Pacific and her islands to far Taboga, where Uncle Sam sends his recuperating children to enjoy the sea baths, hill climbs, and unrivaled pine– apples. It was never my good fortune to get to Taboga. With thirty days' sick leave a year and countless ailments of which I might have been cured free of charge and with the best of care, I could not catch a thing. I had not even the luck of my friend—who, by dint of cross–country runs in the jungle at noonday and similar industrious efforts, worked up at last a temperature of 99 degrees and got his week at Taboga. I stuck immovable at 98.6 degrees.

Soon after five I had bidden Ancon farewell and set off on the last ride across the Isthmus. There was a memory tucked away in every corner. Corozal hotel was still rattling with dishes, Paraiso peeped out from its lap of hills, Culebra with its penitentiary where burglarizing negroes go, sunk away into the past. Railroad Avenue in Empire was still lined with my "enumerated" tags; through an open door I caught a glimpse of a familiar short figure, one foot resting lightly and familiarly on a misapplied gas–pipe, the elbow crooked as if something were held between the fingers. At Bas Obispo I strained my eyes in vain to make out a familiar face in the familiar uniform, there was a glimpse of "Old Fritz" water–gauge as we rumbled across the Chagres, and the train churned away into the heavy green uninhabited night.

Only once more was I aroused, as the lights of Gatun flashed up; then we rolled past the noisy glaring corner of New Gatun and on to Colon. In Cristobal police station I put badge and passes into a heavy envelope and dropped them into the train–guard's box; then turned in for my last night on the Zone. For the steamer already had her fires up that would bear me, and him who was the studious corporal of Miraflores, away in the morning to South America. My police days were ended.

Then a last hand to you all, oh, Z. P. May you live long and continue to do your duty frankly and unafraid. I found you men when I expected only policemen. I reckon my days among you time well spent and I left you regretting that I could stay no longer with you—and when I leave any place with regret it must be possessed of some exceeding subtle charm. But though the world is large, it is also small.

"So I'll meet you later on,
In the place where you have gone,
Where—"

Well, say at San Francisco in 1915, anyway, Hasta luego.

THE END

139

Printed in the United States
113672LV00003B/137-162/A

9 781419 195532